KNOWLEDGE OF GOD
CALVIN, EINSTEIN, AND POLANYI

Author of:
Science, Theology and Einstein, 1982
Science and Theology in Einstein's Perspective, 1986

KNOWLEDGE OF GOD
CALVIN, EINSTEIN, AND POLANYI

IAIN PAUL

SCOTTISH ACADEMIC PRESS
EDINBURGH
1987

Published by
Scottish Academic Press Ltd.
33 Montgomery Street
Edinburgh EH7 5JX

First published 1987
ISBN 0 7073 0537 3

Printed in Great Britain by
Lindsay & Co. Ltd., Edinburgh

CONTENTS

To
James I. McCord and Thomas F. Torrance
in
deep appreciation and gratitude

PREFACE

IF we intend to visit a foreign country for any length of time, we will probably make an effort to learn something of the language of its people. But, when we actually attempt to communicate with them, we will soon find out that the thought-forms of the people are appreciably different from our own in important respects. Therefore, we must also learn about those significant differences in order to enjoy as fully as possible the fellowship of the people. So it may appear to be with the Christian who visits modern science and with the scientist who visits Christian theology. Their common problem seems to be how to speak meaningfully to the supposedly foreign community. Certainly this cannot be done without a basic understanding of the thought-forms of the community. And these will differ slightly from scientific discipline to scientific discipline and more so from scientist to scientist, also from Christian denomination to Christian denomination and more so from theologian to theologian. Nevertheless there are characteristics of modern science and reformed theology which are sufficiently widely recognised and surprisingly closely parallel to be especially considered in this essay. Its primary object is to point to fundamental thought-forms in modern science and reformed theology which can help scientists and theologians to communicate effectively with one another to their mutual benefit. Few theologians will be surprised to find that, in discussing Christian knowing, the theology of John Calvin is selected as the practical foundation of reformed thinking. Equally few scientists will be astonished to discover that the thoughts of Albert Einstein and of Michael Polanyi are chosen as the working bases of scientific thinking. Our essay must be concerned with both practice and theory if we are to understand current trends in scientific and theological thought. Only when this has begun, are we preparing properly for the practical aspects of how to communicate scientific and Christian knowledge in a rapidly changing supertechnological world.

First, we learn that what commands Calvin's unwavering attention is not some abstract knowledge of God but a knowledge of what God is in his relation to ourselves and that the only way to attain this knowledge of God is to study the Scriptures in faith. Unlike purely critical knowledge, faith is a persuasive kind of knowledge. Next, we discover that the one act of Christian knowing engages two distinct but inseparable modes; the activity of the heart is called cordial knowing and the activity of the mind is called intellective knowing. This presentation of Calvin's theology highlights some thought-forms common to Calvin, Einstein, and Polanyi, thus indicating the enduring relevance and the pervasive profundity of the great Reformer's work. In what we may loosely call the experimental section of this essay, we consider some of the available evidence in an effort to identify Calvin's own approach to Scripture and in order to stress the spiritual nature of Christian knowledge or persuasive knowledge. We learn that the doctrine of Scripture is an invariant form of cordial knowledge. This prepares us for a visit to the modern biblical mechanic who reduces unwittingly the biblical material to produce his own literalist truths. With the aid of a simple, concrete example taken from modern science, we run a comparative eye over a typical representation of biblical mechanics, improving our appreciation of the activity of the biblical mechanic and helping us to contrast biblical literalism and Calvin's Christofocal approach. Aspects of the latter are unexpectedly mirrored by the findings of modern geometry.

Calvin is firmly convinced that a proper understanding of Scripture requires more than merely critical reflection and so he prescribes a persuasive apprehension of Scripture which coordinates critical reflection through the guidance of the Holy Spirit. For him, the enlivening meaning and the saving purpose of Christ integrate the form and the content of all biblical statements. We find that Calvin's approach is in tune with some elementary aspects of both the work of the mathematician, Kurt Gödel, and the current mathematical understanding of consistent axiomatisations. Also, we introduce the powerful notion of a biblical isomorphism although we must leave its exciting development for another essay. Then we turn to Calvin's apprehension of the image of God in man in an effort to deepen our appreciation of persuasive knowing as an experience involving the complete personal participation of the individual. His emphasis on the faith of the person receives strong support from the most unlikely source, namely, modern science. Moreover, we can perceive a structural isomorphism between Einstein's thoughts on the practice of science and Calvin's persuasive knowing. Indeed, a fascinating feature of modern science is that it can serve as a parable for the biblical student. This leads us into a discussion of Calvin's openness to the cultural achievements of humankind. The ministry of the Holy Spirit through the instrumentality of modern science should not be denied merely on the basis of creationism or on the strength of fundamentalist modes of human reasoning. In fact, the origins of modern science and of reformed theology share a common basis in faith. The inadequacy of biblical relativism is outlined against the background of some recent thought-provoking advances in modern science with the intention of clarifying the fundamental notion of objective knowledge. This discussion uncovers a novel instructive correspondence between Calvin's theology and Einstein's Special Relativity that indicates the immense significance of the doctrine of Scripture and that promises to reward richly further study.

On investigating persuasive apprehension in relation to Calvin's understanding of the Second Adam, we make a rather strange discovery. The modern scientist appears to work and to know after the pattern of the crucified and risen Lord, although he has no scientific need, and perhaps no particular desire, to recognise this fact. This, of course, supports Calvin's views on the cultural achievements of humankind and it helps us to recognise that persuasive apprehension leads to a growth in wisdom. The immediate relevance of Calvin's work is indicated by a brief discussion of how Christian preaching leads to a persuasive development in Christ, an exercise that reinforces many of the preceding conclusions while signalling the impressive coherence, consistence, and openness of Calvin's theology. We use a knowledge of both persuasive knowing and modern science in order to assess the merits of the powerful role of atomism in modern biblical studies before sketching an open account of Christian knowledge, particularly aspects that are decisive for a real knowledge of God, of self, and of the universe. We conclude that the whole life of the Christian, that is, his complete range of feelings, his entire reach of intelligence, and his full scope of spirit, is enlivened by the Holy Spirit through his articulate heritage as tested by the Word of God. Every increment of this edifying experience is prompted by the Spirit of God, served by the Word of God, and accompanied by an expression of the Person of Christ within the Christian.

I owe my very special gratitude to Rev. Dr. S. W. Peat who read the original manuscript and who cordially supported me with his time and knowledge throughout its preparation. I also wish to express my appreciation to Miss Margaret Maxwell who read the manuscript and made valuable suggestions. I am solely responsible for the errors that remain.

Iain Paul

Pentecost, 1985

CHAPTER 1

KNOWLEDGE OF GOD AND OF OURSELVES

IN the Introduction to his chief work, *The Institutes Of The Christian Religion*,[1] John Calvin declares his basic aim in giving an exposition of Christian doctrine: "It has been my purpose in this labour to prepare and instruct candidates in sacred theology for the reading of the divine Word, in order that they may be able both to have easy access to it and to advance in it without stumbling. For I believe I have so embraced the sum of religion in all its parts, and have arranged it in such an order, that if anyone rightly grasps it, it will not be difficult for him to determine what he ought especially to seek in Scripture, and to what end he ought to relate its contents."[2] Calvin clearly informs the reader that his primary plan is to provide an aid to the study of the Word of God. His intention is to supply what he regards as a necessary part of the equipment of the novice or learner as he proceeds to read Scripture. His book, therefore, is essentially an instrument or a pointer, directing both the seeking and the understanding of the student of Scripture. According to Calvin, in order to seek and to understand what God wishes to teach us in his Word, we require suitable instruction and appropriate direction, for on the basis of human reason alone we are incapable of progressing beyond "foolish" thoughts and "absurd" words.[3] In fact, *The Institutes* opens with an unambiguous declaration of the dual nature of Christian knowing: "Nearly all the wisdom we possess, that is to say, true and sound wisdom, consists of two parts: the knowledge of God and of ourselves."[4] Evidently, Calvin opens his programme of instruction with the very first sentence of his book which directs the reader's attention away from his prior knowledge, and away from his

1

habitual reliance on human reason alone, toward the
fundamental issue of "true and sound" knowledge of God
and of self. Calvin invites his reader to concentrate on the
reality that our knowledge of God is gifted in the same divine
action which enables us to recognise our true persons.

In fact, the Christian's knowledge of God and of self are
so intimately related that it is not easy to discern which one,
if any, precedes and produces the other. As Calvin points
out, there is no knowledge of God without knowledge of
self and no knowledge of self without knowledge of
God.[5] Inevitably, therefore, whoever discusses seriously
knowledge of God will have to discuss at some subsequent
stage knowledge of self. But this perplexing prospect appears
strangely familiar. Indeed, it recalls a modern argument
from Michael Polanyi's *Lindsay Memorial Lectures* on *The
Study of Man*[6] in which he discusses the problem of understanding man. The words Polanyi used then need only slight
adaptation now, for they capture aptly the dilemma of the
apparently unending effort of trying to grasp any kind of
purely critical, comprehensive knowledge. Thus, we may
say, in agreement with Calvin but in Polanyi's language,
authentic knowledge of God and of self must involve more
than merely critical knowledge, for "as soon as we had
completed one such study, our subject matter would have
been extended by this very achievement. We should have
now to study the study that we had just completed, since it,
too, would be a work of [God and of self]. And so we should
have to go on reflecting ever again on our last reflections, in
an endless and futile endeavour to comprise completely the
works of [God and of self]".[6] Although they were separated
by four centuries and by excellence in different disciplines,
Calvin the theologian and Polanyi the scientist obviously
shared common insights about the nature of human
knowing, a circumstance which points us refreshingly to the
continued relevance of Calvin's theological works in our
supertechnological world.

Our dilemma about critical knowledge is what we choose
to call a Polanyian difficulty. To some people it may appear
far-fetched, but it suggests to us that there is ample

justification for a careful reconsideration of the theological usefulness of exclusively critical knowledge to the post-critical, late-twentieth century mind. If the Christian decides to rely solely on his own logical resources in the attempt to grasp objective knowledge of God and of self, then Polanyi's description is singularly appropriate: "the moment he reflects on his own knowledge he catches himself red-handed in the act of upholding his knowledge. He finds himself asserting it to be true, and this asserting and believing is an action which makes an addition to the subject on which his knowledge bears."[7] So every time we acquire knowledge, we enlarge our subject by something that is not yet incorporated in the knowledge we hold, and in this sense a comprehensive knowledge of God and of self must appear impossible. This chasing of our critical tails signals for us the need to explore the possibility that there is more to the nature of human knowing than merely following our own words.

Actually, Calvin is not concerned with neutral or detached observations, or with intellectual speculations, about the existence and the nature of God, whose essence is incomprehensible and whose divineness far escapes all human perception.[8] He is fully aware that, if we try to draw God closer to us by our sensible representations, we are failing to recognise the incomprehensibility of God and we are refusing to acknowledge the ineffable separation of God from his creatures.[9] Calvin shows little interest in the idea of man knowing that God is without knowing what God is, or in the thought of man knowing what God is without experiencing communion with God. What commands the unwavering attention of Calvin is not some abstract knowledge about God but a knowledge of who God is in his relation to ourselves. He believes that humankind has an innate knowledge of God which is awakened and exercised by the gracious revelation of God both in nature and in providence. However, fallen man cannot respond properly to this manifestation and so, in Calvin's view, it became necessary to provide through the Scriptures an objective revelation of God. Thus the only way to attain this knowledge of God is to study the Scriptures. They alone can reveal to us what we can and ought to know of the existence and nature of God,[10] assuming of course that we have the necessary faith to apprehend his mysteries.[11] But faith involves more than an explicit appeal to the intellect. It is a gift from God and "the only true faith is that which the Spirit of God seals in our hearts".[11] The Spirit of God transforms the whole person of the sinful individual enabling him to receive this revelation. The mind, the feeling, and the willing of the person are transfigured by the operation of the Holy Spirit. Calvin believes firmly that the "same Spirit, therefore, who has spoken through the mouths of the prophets must penetrate into our hearts to persuade us that they faithfully proclaimed what had been divinely commanded".[12] The persuasive truth of Scripture is mysteriously self-evident. Consequently, our belief in the Scriptures as the objective revelation of God springs from a source other than mere human reason. Indeed, "we ought to seek our conviction in a higher place than human reasons, judgments, or conjectures, that is in the secret testimony of the Spirit".[12] The conjoint action of the objective revelation of God and of the personal guidance of the Spirit of God communicates a "true and sound" wisdom to the person.

Even this scanty sketch of Calvin's approach to human knowing is sufficient to show that he is a thoroughly modern thinker. Specifically, we are attracted by his keen awareness of the importance of the inseparability of the two components of knowledge, the divine and the human, an awareness which focuses on the mystery of the Incarnation and, therefore, which is Christofocal. We note that the objective revelation of God is God addressing us in human words as, simultaneously, the Spirit of God ministers to our person. Both aspects of the same divine action reflect the mystery of the Word who became flesh and dwelt among us. Whereas Calvin the theologian is alive to the incarnational mystery of the Gospel and its pervasive power, Albert Einstein the scientist is alert to the scientific mystery of the intelligibility of the natural order. He describes the fundamental problem of modern scientific research as "the eternal antithesis between the two inseparable components of knowledge, the empirical and the rational''.[13] Einstein accommodates this intelligibility by recognising that the rationality of the universe is the universe disclosing itself to us in ordered phenomena as, simultaneously, the *intuendum* confronting the scientist prepares him to apprehend those disclosures. By the word *intuendum* we mean the thing intuited or the thing to be intuited by the scientist. The underlying assumption is that the objective world plays an active role by making compelling claims on the scientific mind. Thus Einstein is able to resolve the apparent tension between the logically free creation of a scientific concept and the attribution to it of a real existence independent of the sense impressions that gave rise to it. He does so by recognising that conceptual systems are empirically loaded.[14] In other words, the *intuendum* of the scientist mysteriously schools him in the ways of the universe and the formulations of scientific theory are influenced by the facts known to their originators. Also, Einstein regards scientific facts as theory-laden.[14] This means, of course, that the precise observational or experimental determination of scientific facts is dependent upon current scientific theory. Possibly it comes as a great surprise to many people to learn that Einstein himself could hold such unproven and unprovable beliefs. Yet, when we come to think of it, it is readily appreciated that the reality, the rationality, and the intelligibility of the universe cannot be proved. The modern scientist must believe in them in order to understand the universe. The plain fact is that unprovable beliefs lie at the basis of all knowledge. Indeed, Einstein acknowledges freely that belief in an external world independent of the observer is the foundation of all science.[15] He also believes that the *intuendum* schools personal assessment enabling scientists to pursue their commitment to the scientific enterprise.[16] Remarkably, in order to serve the mystery of scientific knowledge, Einstein talks of the empirical and the rational, of the rationality and the intelligibility of the universe, and of things intuited and of a growing sympathy with the natural order, whereas, in order to accommodate the mystery of theological knowledge, Calvin relates in terms of the divine and the human, of the revelation of God and the Spirit of God, and of inspiration and a developing faith. This extended similarity in the independent ideas of two deservedly renowned thinkers, who are so widely separated in time and apparently in discipline, suggests that they may share deep common conceptual roots. At the very least, it supports the contention that Calvin's theology is relevant in an age that picks so many of the fruits of modern science without recognising even the basic faith of the scientist.

Perhaps we should not be too hasty in our condemnation of those who do not recognise the basic faith of the scientist, for in condemning others we may well find that we are also condemning ourselves. Are we so sure that we hold a proper appreciation of the nature of Christian faith? Calvin informs us that the faith, which the Spirit of God alone initiates, is "the inward persuasion of the Holy Spirit".[17] This persuasion involves the whole person. It is a persuasion of the mind and of the heart which brings the individual to a personal relationship with God in Jesus Christ and which carries him to a sound conviction about the divine origin and authority of Scripture. Such a persuasion is more than intellectual assent. For Calvin, faith is "a firm and certain knowledge of God's benevolence toward us, founded upon the truth of the freely given promise in Christ, both revealed to our minds and sealed upon our hearts through the Holy Spirit".[18] Here we have a rather unusual association of concepts. Calvin informs us in the same breath, as it were, that faith is a kind of knowledge and that the one act of human knowing engages two distinct but inseparable modes. If we understand Calvin correctly, then he is telling us that in the act of human knowing there is both an activity of the heart, cordial knowing, and an activity of the mind, intellective knowing, and that the persuasion of the Holy Spirit schools simultaneously the two distinct modes of human knowing. As Calvin puts it, the Holy Spirit reveals knowledge to the human mind but seals it in the human heart. The obvious implication seems to be that knowledge of the heart is intrinsically unformalisable, because cordial knowledge lies beyond the mind. It is none the less suprarational, because it is communicated by the Holy Spirit. The logical knowledge of the mind is familiar to all, although Calvin presents us with the profound notions that intellective knowledge is instrumental to and transformed by the Holy Spirit. In Calvin's view, faith is persuasive knowledge which has two distinct but inseparable modes of knowing as does all human knowing. Persuasive knowledge is "not merely a question of knowing that God exists, but also — and this especially — of knowing what is his will toward us".[19] Thus we can understand how the personal or relational aspects of faith are "more strengthened by the persuasion of divine truth than instructed by rational proof",[20] for "faith is the principal work of the Holy Spirit"[21] who can uniquely minister within us to the two distinct modes of the one act of human knowing.

Recognising the antithesis between the holiness of all that is divine and the sinfulness of all that is human, Calvin could only rely on the ultimate mystery that God was in Christ reconciling the world to himself in order to relate appropriately to the divine and to the human in all Christian knowledge. Foremost in Calvin's heart and mind is the reality that the Incarnation is the way including the pattern, the truth imparting the content, and the life providing the dynamics, of all genuine theological inquiry. But we have just observed how Einstein handles the inseparability of the empirical and the rational by recognising that scientific facts are theory-laden and scientific theories are empirically loaded. Clearly, Calvin approaches the antithesis between the two inseparable components of knowledge, the divine and the human, in a remarkably similar fashion. According to Calvin, if the person has the faith to apprehend the mysteries of God and of self, then he recognises that through the Holy Spirit the human word is 'divinely invested' and the divine Word is 'humanly accommodating'. As is only to be expected of a great theologian, we find the Word incarnate, and therefore the doctrine of the Holy Trinity, at the very heart of Calvin's theology. Whenever Calvin writes of "the inward persuasion of the Holy Spirit", he is referring to the one action of the indwelling Word of God who grounds our personal knowledge of the mind and of the heart in the objective revelation of God.

The solution to our Polanyian difficulty, our logical oddity, seems to lie in the fact that Calvin distinguishes two kinds of human knowledge. What is usually described as human knowledge is formulated and communicable. It is what Calvin calls knowledge of the mind. But knowledge of the mind is not the only kind of human knowledge. Unformulated knowledge, called knowledge of the heart by Calvin,[20] is another form of human knowledge. This second form is not just hazy and vague. It is unspecifiable because it can never be made explicit. Like Polanyi, but centuries before him, Calvin solves our logical oddity by recognising that the formulated knowledge of speech, books etc., is explicit knowledge which can serve as logical and descriptive knowledge. But Calvin realises that explicit knowledge can also be signitive, that is, it can be a sign pointing to things beyond itself without describing or demonstrating them. Since only a passing acquaintance with the Ten Commandments is sufficient to indicate that theological concepts are not interchangeable with the realities of God to which they refer, we can readily grasp Calvin's point that their function must include serving the truth as they bear witness to God. For Calvin, explicit theological knowledge is signitive and intellective, unspecifiable theological knowledge is cordial, and there is a whole word of difference between ordinary human knowing and the persuasion of the Holy Spirit. This difference is discussed more fully elsewhere [chapter 5]. Here we limit ourselves to the simple declaration that Calvin believes that the two modes of human knowing, knowledge of the heart and of the mind, are only correctly integrated by the persuasion of the Holy Spirit. Consequently, genuine knowledge of God is persuasive knowledge involving a proper coordination of the two modes of human knowing. In such a coordination, the function of knowledge of the heart is to orient properly knowledge of the mind and the role of knowledge of the mind is to point to knowledge of the heart. But our knowledge of the heart is rooted in the divinely invested Scriptures and grounded in the humanly accommodating experience of God. So our unspecifiable knowledge represents a far greater harmony with the Word of God than our explicit theological concepts can possibly express even if they could correspond formally with its literal truth.[21] This means that, according to Calvin, all genuinely theological concepts are necessarily signitive, although they may also have authentic descriptive or demonstrative functions.

In order to appreciate more fully the profundity, power, and permanence of Calvin's theology, we compare it briefly with relevant aspects of the thought of Polanyi on the nature of modern scientific inquiry. From his own experience and knowledge of scientific research, Polanyi recognises that what he calls the objectivist account of scientific inquiry is strikingly at odds with the real nature of modern science and its working methods. According to the objectivists, the procedures for establishing and upholding scientific knowledge rely on the application of exact and precise methods that can be formally described. Those methods do not require any element of personal judgment that involves the passions of the scientist or that relies on his intuition or on any other unspecifiable skill or faculty. In his book *Personal Knowledge* and in his other writings, Polanyi exposes this kind of totally detached 'objectivity' as a delusion that exercises a destructive influence within science and that "falsifies our whole outlook far beyond the domain of science".[22]

Polanyi's rejection of the objectivist account is not just an academic exercise. On the contrary, it is firmly based on his extensive working knowledge of modern science. He has learned in the laboratory that the most significant procedures of scientific inquiry are not governed by formal rules. For example, in discovery, in the relation of facts to theories, and in the discernment of a suitable research project, the personal judgments of the scientist are guided by intuition and they deploy his practical skills, his intellectual equipment, and his individual expertise, his commitments, and his emotions. Obviously, such personal judgments must always leave some residual indeterminacies which cannot be legitimately ignored. In other words, there are irreducibly personal judgments at work in all scientific research. Indeed, those very judgments have an indispensable objectivity that springs from the scientist's obedience to the disclosures of the natural order. Following Einstein, Polanyi argues that the intuitive grasp of real coherences in nature by mathematical reasoning allows the scientist to transcend sensory perception.[23] Specifically, he states that "any critical verification of a scientific statement requires the same powers for recognising rationality in nature as does the process of scientific discovery, even though it exercises these at a lower level".[24] Thus, the discovery of objective scientific knowledge, or to a lesser extent the critical verification of that knowledge, brings into play an "apprehension of rationality which commands our respect and arouses our contemplative admiration".[25] Scientific discovery, "while using our senses as clues, transcends this experience by embracing the vision of a reality beyond the impressions of our senses, a vision which speaks for itself in guiding us to an ever deeper understanding of reality".[25] Here we find Polanyi struggling to express the mystery that reality seems to speak for itself and with a rationality that is somehow sufficiently intelligible to humankind. It is apparent that Polanyi sensed the need for the word *intuendum*.

Polanyi argues that all inquiry is grounded in personal judgments which have both a passionate element and an unformalisable element, [recall Calvin's knowledge of the mind and of the heart]. In his development of their structure he introduces what he calls tacit knowing. His reconsideration of human knowledge starts from the fundamental fact that "we can know more than we can tell".[26] An interesting experiment that shows clearly what he means by this statement concerns the phenomenon of subception as studied by R. S. Lazarus and R. A. McCleary.[27] In this experiment a large number of nonsense syllables were presented to a particular subject, followed by the administration of an electric shock. When the procedure was repeated, the person quickly reacted to what was happening and, on seeing the shock syllables, he anticipated the shocks. But when the scientists asked the subject how he knew when the shock was coming, he could not tell them. Somehow he had come to know when to expect a shock, but he could not tell what made him expect it. The subject had acquired a knowledge similar to the knowledge we have of a person who we recognise by certain signs although we cannot tell exactly what those signs are. On the basis of a knowledge of this kind drawn from his extensive experience of modern science, Polanyi distinguishes two kinds of knowledge. The first kind of knowledge is explicit and includes articulated concepts and mathematical formulae. The second kind is what Polanyi calls tacit knowledge. It covers all of our unformulated knowledge, our implicit and unspecifiable knowledge. According to Polanyi, in tacit knowing we always attend from something in order to attend to something else. For example, Polanyi would probably agree that we always attend from our theological concepts in order to attend to Jesus Christ. And Calvin would surely see this as another way of saying that our theological concepts are necessarily signitive of Jesus Christ whom we know with our hearts as well as with our minds. Therefore, we draw the exciting conclusion that, although they were separated by centuries, the contributions of Calvin and of Polanyi show remarkable similarities, which must not, however, blind us to their important differences.

We recall that Calvin presents *The Institutes* as an instrument that points out what we should search for in Scripture and that indicates to what end we should relate the contents of Scripture. His stated intentions make it perfectly clear that he certainly does not offer his chief theological work as a purely critical or merely descriptive substitute either for the Bible or for its true end, Jesus Christ. On the contrary, from what we can gather of Calvin's under-standing of persuasive knowing, we must assume that he believes the principal underlying purpose of all authentic theological endeavours to be the advancement of the reader's firm intention of finding Jesus Christ through the proper study of the Scriptures. In fact, Calvin assures us staunchly in *The Institutes* that "holy men of old knew God only by beholding him in his Son as in a mirror (cf. II Cor. 3: 18). When I say this, I mean that God has never manifested himself to men in any other way than through the Son, that is, his sole wisdom, light, and truth. From this fountain Adam, Noah, Abraham, Isaac, Jacob, and others drank all that they had of heavenly teaching. From the same fountain, all the prophets have also drawn every heavenly oracle that they have given forth."[28] This assurance is unambiguously Christofocal. It is based on the reality that Jesus Christ is the beginning and the end of the Scriptures. And, in case we harbour any lingering doubts, Calvin goes on to remind us that the apostles were, of course, among those who drank from this very fountain, experiencing "Christ's Spirit as precursor in a certain measure dictating the words"[29] which we now know as the Gospel.

If Jesus Christ is the heart of the Bible, which he surely is to all his followers, and if all Scripture points to him as the vivifying knowledge of God, which Calvin firmly believes, then all genuine Christian knowing is based on the persuasive integration of the two modes of human knowing. As we have already noted, this integration imparts a signitive role to theological knowledge and an orienting function to cordial knowledge. All authentic theological words and statements are necessarily ostensive. They direct us away from themselves through our cordial knowledge to him who is the only image of the invisible God.[30] If they do otherwise, then they are being deflected by an ulterior purpose and so they cannot converge on Christ, the unique focus of all knowledge of God and of self. Instead, they are abandoned to some self-reliant form of human knowing and its intrinsic deficiencies in the coordination between tacit and explicit knowing. In short, they have fallen an easy prey to the timeless tendency of humankind to make idols of their artifacts. Borrowing from Calvin's commentary on Hebrews, we may say that theological words and statements "in vain weary themselves in serving God, except they observe the right way, and that all religions are not only vain, but also pernicious, with which the true and certain knowledge of God is not connected; for all are prohibited from having any access to God, who do not distinguish and separate him from idols; in short, there is no religion, except where this truth reigns dominant.''[31] Like Calvin, we recognise that we are not creators of the true and certain knowledge of God. Neither are we controllers of this truth nor manipulators of it. Indeed, we acknowledge that there is only one proper role for our explicit knowledge to play if we are to have access to God. This role is to point to the truth of which we are solidly persuaded. Our theological concepts must not come between us and the truth. They must not detract in any way from the truth. Their primary role is to serve the truth. Therefore, we depend upon our cordial knowledge to ensure that our theological words and statements are instrumental. In so far as those words and statements are signposts guiding the spiritual traveller in the right direction, our theological utterances are inherently practical and coherently translucent.

So far our attention has been essentially confined to biblical knowledge, almost as if all other forms of knowledge are relatively unimportant to Calvin. In fact, Calvin draws on all kinds of knowledge throughout his extensive writings. He makes good use of his extra-biblical knowledge but this knowledge is never allowed to eclipse or to obscure the one and only end of his theology. His aim is to make intelligible to us the revelation of God in Jesus Christ who is the unique truth in whom the Person and the Word are inseparably one, and in whom human knowing is actually persuasive knowing since in him the two modes of knowing are never uncoordinated or disintegrated by sin. The Person of Christ reveals that the Word of God surpasses all conceptual systems and, therefore, all objectivist knowledge of the mind. The Word of God discloses that the Person of Christ transcends all personalism and, therefore, all subjectivist knowledge of the heart. Uniquely the revelation of God in Jesus Christ presents us with the inseparability of the objective and the personal. The dual nature of this truth means that we can receive the Word of God only in personal relation to Christ and that there can be no communion with

Christ apart from some communication of the Word of God. In the theology-soaked words of Calvin, true knowledge of God and of self is offered to us by God the Father in Christ clothed with his Gospel.[19] With those few observations we have only removed the strings from the profoundly Christofocal, theological package which Calvin sends us across the centuries. In fact, he invites us to establish the authenticity of all theological statements by objectively grounding them in the Word of God and by personally anchoring them in Christ. All truly Christian knowing of God and of self springs ultimately from the unity of the divinely invested Word of God and of the humanly accommodating Word of God. This means that all genuinely theological knowledge is the communication of real practical knowledge that coheres in Jesus Christ, and that guides the daily life of the Christian. But, if all theology is practical, then we neglect aspects of it at our peril.

Although the truth is disclosed to us, we can always resist true knowledge of God and of self. On encountering the persuasive truth, we discover that we are at variance with it. In fundamental respects, our human knowing is closed in upon itself. Instead of recognising the objective revelation of God, we tend to objectify our inadequate counterfeits. Rather than experience personal transformation in Christ, we prefer to indulge in subjectivism. The resulting, contrived coordination of our unspecifiable and explicit knowledge separates us from a true knowledge of God. The openness of this truth toward us is opposed by our estranged wills, our entrenched desires, our established habits, our rebellious thoughts, and our discordant words. Yet we are always invited by the persuasive truth to allow our thoughts, words, and actions to be directed along our personal, objective life in Christ. In reality, our free obedience to God's will is the only response that can lead to our release from the unbearable yoke of the law,[32] which emprisons us spiritually in the solitary confinement of distintegrated living and knowing. Because Jesus Christ has fulfilled the requirements of the law, God accepts mercifully our inadequate obedience. He judges us graciously after the perfect obedience of Christ rather than according to our incomplete and imperfect achievements in thought, word, and deed. Time and time again, we are lovingly called as inveterate, but redeemed, sinners throughout the length and breadth, the height and depth, of our lives to walk in the freedom of the children of God.

As Calvin writes, Christians "are taught to live not according to their own whims but according to God's will".[33] This means that we need to deny ourselves in order to benefit from the persuasive truth. Such denials cannot be confined to the merely critical aspects of our thought for that would do nothing to solve the primary problems of uncoordinated knowing and of distintegrated living. Wherever necessary we must be prepared to abandon our conceptual inventions, conventions, and declensions. Our habits, preferences, and desires drive us to fashion the truth after our own satisfactions and intentions. As they are thoroughly exposed by Christ, we are inevitably offended because both the extent and the intent of our apostasy are disconcertingly disclosed. Yet the way of persuasive truth opens for us the path of recognition, humility, and surrender through repentance and self-denial. As Calvin himself says, "he alone has duly denied himself who has so totally resigned himself to the Lord that he permits every part of his life to be governed by God's will."[34] Because sinful humankind is existentially severed from the truth, it needs to be reconciled to God; that is, the whole life of the individual has to be resigned to him. As we yield our complete beings in repentant obedience before the persuasive truth, our human knowing is conformed to the rational activity of God's self-revelation and it becomes persuasive knowing.

Obedience, humility, and self-denial are not strangers to the scientific enterprise. This is shown by a brief consideration of an intriguing scientific problem. In scientific research new aspects of reality are often postulated. But, as Polanyi asks, how "can we guess the presence of a real relationship between observed data, if its existence has never before been known"?[35] In search of an answer to this question, Polanyi turns to "the process by which we usually first establish the reality of certain things around us. Our principal clue to the reality of an object is its possession of a coherent outline. . . . We can say, therefore, that the capacity of scientists to guess the presence of shapes as tokens of reality differs from the capacity of our ordinary perception, only by the fact that it can integrate shapes presented to it in terms which the perception of ordinary people cannot readily handle. The scientist's intuition can integrate widely dispersed data, camouflaged by sundry irrelevant connexions, and indeed seek out such data by experiments guided by a dim foreknowledge of the possibilities which lie ahead. These perceptions may be erroneous; just as the shape of a camouflaged body may be erroneously perceived in everyday life." [35]

According to Polanyi, "the capacity of scientists to guess the presence of shapes as tokens of reality" depends upon their intuition which integrates "widely dispersed data". In other words, Polanyi closely follows Einstein in relying on the thing intuited by the scientist to develop a growing sympathy with the natural order. Interestingly, both men talk of scientific discovery in terms of the intuitive integration of the researcher's fragmented knowing, terms that seem to mirror our apprehension of Calvin's persuasive knowing. A crucial difference, however, separates the three thinkers, one which it would be iniquitous to ignore. Einstein and Polanyi believe that the initiative in scientific discovery is taken by the Reason that manifests itself in nature. They indicate that they know that God is but they do not pursue a knowledge of who God is in relation to us. They cope with the mystery of scientific discovery without direct reference to that Reason. By contrast, Calvin never dissociates persuasive knowing from the Holy Spirit. If in their thinking Einstein and Polanyi are 'cosmocentric', Calvin is Christofocal. Yet he indicates that disordered human knowing is anthropocentric, and so its variant, 'cosmocentrism', would be new to him in name only.

Scientific cosmocentrism identifies obedience, humility, and self-denial as the trusted companions of the gifted scientific researcher. Polanyi obviously believes that there is a structural kinship between perception and scientific discovery. It takes the form of the integration of clues into a coherent entity. Sometimes such an integration involves no new data, but rather associates already known data in novel and original ways. The mark of scientific genius is, for Polanyi, the ability to apprehend new coherences where other scientists do not. This gift is a faculty that is necessarily obedient to the disclosures of reality. It requires humility for it is invariably guided by the *intuendum*. In the absence of self-denial, this gift is not responsibly equipped to depart from established patterns of apprehension. But, as the humble scientist yields his complete expertise in expectant obedience before his intuitive hunch, his rational activity is transformed by the presence of the real coherences of nature and he makes a discovery.

Persuasive knowing will only occur during theological activity if reconciliation takes place. A new coordination of human knowing must be experienced as part of a new objective and personal relation to Christ. This personal oneness of growing and knowing in Christ is free from both the coercive power and the paralysing curse of the law that every disobedient word or act entails.[36] As obedient servants, we are not bound to the curse and the compulsion of the law. We relate to its inner content or its command of love.[37] We know that God is pleased to accept our services for the sake of Christ, and so our thoughts, utterances, and actions have a Christofocal dynamics. Such things as inflexible standards, rigid systems, exact schedules, or precise regulations certainly have limited applications in both Christian living and knowing, but they do not dominate the imperfect, incomplete, and frail efforts of those who are willing and obedient. In Christ, God has made all things ours. Therefore, we are not under any obligation about formal observances or stereotyped performances which, in themselves, are matters of indifference. Like the modern scientist, we are free to use or to ignore conventional procedures and standard practices as we choose.[38] For we go through life in Christ continually rediscovering the openness of mind and of heart that breaks us out of the narrowing confines of fear and habit. Through his Spirit we experience daily the revealing, reconciling, and vivifying knowledge of the revelation of God in Jesus Christ.

Following the biblical rejection of all forms of idolatry, and therefore of all kinds of slavery, formulated theological knowledge is primarily signitive. Such explicit knowledge seeks always to avoid anything that appears to bring God within the manipulative grasp of the imagination. While it may describe and demonstrate certain aspects of the things of God, its primary function is to point beyond itself to cordial knowledge of God and of self. Genuine theological knowledge strives to eliminate everything that would encourage interest in it as anything other than signitive.[39] According to Calvin, unformulated, unspecifiable knowledge, cordial knowledge, arises as the Christian searches the Word of God under the guidance of the Holy Spirit.[11] Cordial knowledge is suprarational, humanly incommunicable knowledge. Thus persuasive knowledge, that is, the inseparable coordination or divine integration of cordial and theological knowledge, is enlivening knowledge of Jesus Christ. It is revealing and reconciling. We can say in Polanyian style that we always know persuasively that our intellective knowledge directs us through our cordial knowledge to the truth. If we are willing to hold our explicit Christian knowledge primarily as intellective knowledge, then it can function as the medium of our listening and communicating and of our obeying and serving, and the vain pursuit of reflecting ever again on our own reflections no longer arises. This problem only occurs when we choose to hold our explicit Christian knowledge as exclusively critical, comprehensive knowledge, that is, as articulated knowledge without unspecifiable remainder.

To paraphrase Polanyi's profound observations,[40] the question is whether we are willing to hold our explicit Christian knowledge primarily as intellective knowledge. On the one hand, there is always the imaginative tendency to transform intellective knowledge into a possession to be controlled and manipulated. Merely descriptive or demonstrative knowledge can be handled readily in this way. On the other hand, cordial knowledge seems to be subjective, apparently lacking the public objective character of explicit knowledge that is the essential quality of knowledge. This objection should not be lightly dismissed, but it is mistaken. Participation of the person in the shaping of Christian knowledge of God and of self does not invalidate that knowledge. It requires an understanding of objectivity that differs markedly from the traditional one. This essay attempts to transmit this conviction. It also tries to show that persuasive knowledge is in fact the dominant principle of all Christian knowledge by drawing mainly on the thoughts of John Calvin, Albert Einstein, Kurt Gödel, and Michael Polanyi. The rejection of persuasive knowledge automatically involves the impairment of any Christian knowledge whatever. We must try to demonstrate, therefore, that the personal participation through which the knowledge of the Christian is shaped necessarily predominates at all levels of Christian knowing, although the decisive role of persuasive knowledge is not generally recognised in Christian theology.

Chapter 2

CALVIN AND SCRIPTURE

IN order to highlight the spiritual nature of persuasive knowledge, we now consider in detail some aspects of Calvin's approach to the Scriptures. This allows us to contrast, for example, the unformulated, cordial knowledge and the explicit, intellective knowledge of the Christian. At the outset and as a step of sheer faith, we avow that the kind of unspecifiable knowledge which we receive through the ministry of the Holy Spirit on reading the Word of God is incomparably richer than mere human reason.[41] In fact, the richness of cordial knowledge is the source of the limited rational content of our explicit Christian knowledge. Also, we accept that an essential rational difference between cordial and intellective knowledge is that we can critically reflect on something explicitly stated or written in a way in which we cannot and need not reflect on our cordial awareness of the enlivening Christ. Critical reflection has, of course, a role to play in Christian endeavour, but it is necessarily a subservient function. To give to it a comprehensive role is to mistake a part for the whole. A contrived framework of interpretation would then inevitably deprive our theological knowledge of its proper content by eclipsing its real centre and, therefore, its true meaning.[42] This abuse of critical reflection insinuates subtle irrationalities into the minds of Christians by transforming the unspecifiable into the unknowable and the intellective into the definitive. The crucial point is that we can always justifiably doubt our human reasoning but not our cordial knowledge, for with the latter the divine element is active and dominant.

Hopefully, the tremendous importance of this particular difference will become obvious as we contrast a persuasive apprehension of the Bible and the much more familiar definitive understanding of the Scriptures known as biblical inerrancy. Our discussion of the former takes the concrete form of Calvin's treatment of the biblical corpus. This provides us with a tangible illustration against which we can bring into sharp relief dangerous abuses of the Scriptures which arise so easily from a misguided dependence upon supposedly pure, critical knowledge. It also gives a topical edge to our deliberations, showing that Calvin's studies still have much to offer modern generations of Christians. Certainly, from this exercise, we learn something of the limited nature of critical reflection as we heighten our awareness of the divine mystery of biblical inspiration. Since the contention that Calvin adheres to the high doctrine of the plenary verbal inspiration of Scripture currently emanates from the four points of the compass, now seems to be an opportune time to reconsider certain frequently quoted passages in his voluminous works. We are referring, of course, to those which appear to support directly the assertion that God selected both the definitive ideas and the specific words of Scripture in order to describe and to demonstrate the truth for humankind. Any responsible assessment of biblical inerrancy will naturally include a serious consideration of those passages. But the choice of their translations will remain open to question, unless we are prepared to accept the work of a distinguished scholar who is also a champion of biblical inerrancy. Consequently, in order to obviate a charge of playing with words, we readily accept, for the purposes of our discussion of biblical inspiration, the easily accessible translations of John Murray,[43] an eminent Calvin scholar. Hopefully, since he claims that his renderings of various relevant passages are pointed and accurate, misgivings about translations can be minimised, if not eliminated.

It is no surprise to find out that *The Institutes* yields several notable pronouncements on the nature of Scripture which demand the attention of every diligent student of Calvin. For example, not far into this classic work we read: ''Whether God revealed himself to the fathers by oracles and visions, or, by the instrumentality and ministry of men, suggested what they were to hand down to posterity, there cannot be a doubt that the certainty of what he taught them was firmly engraven on their hearts, so that they felt assured and knew that the things which they learnt came forth from God, who invariably accompanied his Word with a sure testimony, infinitely superior to mere opinion. . . . For if we reflect how prone the human mind is to forgetfulness of God, how readily inclined to every kind of error, how bent every now and then on devising new and fictitious religions, it will be easy to understand how necessary it was to make such a depository of doctrine as would secure it from either perishing by the neglect, vanishing amid the errors, or being corrupted by the presumptuous audacity of men.''[44]

Here Calvin claims that the inscripturation of heavenly doctrine was necessary to guard against the neglect, error, and audacity of humankind. But, when you have a mind that is as astute as Calvin's mind, you are fully acquainted with the fact that the sole provision of a set of word-perfect documents is not an adequate safeguard against the neglect, error, or corruption of human agencies. Whether the Scriptures are word-perfect or not, they have always been, and always will be, open to the ravages of humankind. Therefore, if the priority is to maintain word-perfection, then some form of continuous protection has to be operative. But Calvin does not refer to such an unbroken provision. So we can reasonably assume that he is concerned about something other than the verbal precision of the Scriptures. Significantly, in this passage, Calvin writes of a certainty of knowledge that derives from God ''who invariably accompanied his Word with a sure testimony, infinitely superior to mere opinion''. He is deliberately contrasting the certainty of knowledge of the heart and the frailty of knowledge of the mind in order to emphasise the importance of an accompanying ''sure testimony''. Similarly, Calvin stresses the different roles of the human and the divine in the one act of biblical inspiration. On the human side, we have the media of oracles and visions and also the instrumentality and ministry of men, and on the divine side, there is the accompanying, suggesting, teaching, "sure testimony" of God. Elsewhere, Calvin amplifies this cardinal concept by referring to it as "the secret testimony of the Spirit".[12] One thing, at least, is clear from this passage. Calvin recognises that the real mystery of biblical inspiration is the intelligibility of the Voice of God. In fact, he believes firmly that "the depository of doctrine" results from this inseparability of the human and the divine. Moreover, he writes specifically that it is this depository that is secured from neglect, error, and corruption. Since Calvin refers to a knowledge of the heart, and since cordial knowledge is immune to the errors of the human mind, could it be that he regards this depository as an invariant form of cordial knowledge that is accessible only by reading the Scriptures as guided by the Holy Spirit? Clearly, whatever else Calvin means by "the depository of doctrine", this passage consistently points us beyond meagre human artifacts to the activity of God clothed in earthly things.

In the following chapter of *The Institutes,* Calvin addresses the delicate subject of the authority of Scripture: "since no daily oracles are given from heaven, and the Scriptures alone exist as the means by which God has been pleased to consign his truth to perpetual remembrance, the full authority which they obtain with the faithful proceeds from no other consideration than that they are persuaded that they proceeded from heaven, as if God had been giving utterance to them."[45] According to Calvin, the Scriptures are not themselves the truth, but only "the means" by which God has consigned the truth to perpetual remembrance. In other words, they are uniquely instrumental to the truth, serving it with an authority that comes from God himself. Since only the faithful are persuaded of this authority, they alone are guided to treat the Scriptures as if God uttered them. But, because God does not cheat humankind by substituting some form of divine communication in the appearance of human words, Christians know persuasively; that is, they are persuaded by both cordial and intellective knowledge, that the truth of God for humankind employs but transcends human words.

It is not, therefore, the words that capture the truth, but the truth that embraces the words.

In fact, only a few sections later, Calvin writes: "Scripture is from God, but in a way that surpasses human judgment, we are perfectly assured . . . that it has come to us by the ministry of men from the very mouth of God. . . . We feel the firmest conviction that we hold an invincible truth."[46] Of course we hold "an invincible truth", but only in so far as God allows us to do so. The frailty of human reasoning reminds Calvin and us just how much we need to be "perfectly assured". Our assurance must come in "a way that surpasses human judgment" but in a manner that does not dispense with human reasoning. Indeed, the truth has come to us "by the ministry of men from the very mouth of God". Calvin makes it crystal clear that solid conviction about "invincible truth" cannot rest on mere human reason. He also points carefully to the instrumentality of men, knowing that the human word is insufficient in itself to convey the truth. As on so many other occasions, Calvin finds it necessary to refer to the inseparability of the human and the divine in order to express his thoughts adequately. Here he does so in terms of the indivisibility of "the ministry of men from the very mouth of God".

In the fourth book of *The Institutes* Calvin writes: "Between the apostles and their successors, however, there is, as I have stated, this difference that the apostles were the certain and authentic amanuenses of the Holy Spirit and therefore their writings are to be received as the oracles of God, but others have no other office than to teach what is revealed and deposited in the holy Scriptures."[47] Obviously Calvin knows that things are normally "deposited" in a containing vessel or medium and, as we have already noted, this is not an unique reference to the notion of a "deposit". We may justifiably assume, therefore, that he is referring here to the depository of the doctrine of Scripture in the medium of the human word. Again, we are made aware that Calvin sees two inseparable elements at work in the divine mystery of biblical inspiration. On this occasion he describes the cooperation of the human and the divine as the apostles being the amanuenses of the Holy Spirit. Also, he points out that, whereas the office of apostle includes instrumental writing, the office of teacher is confined to what is "revealed and deposited in the holy Scriptures". In other words, authentic teachers depend on both inspiration and revelation for their apprehension of the Scriptures. True teachers rely on the personal guidance of the Holy Spirit as they relate to the objective Word of God, recognising that human reason alone is utterly inadequate. The difference between apostles and teachers is only one of office or instrumentality for the two groups experience the same intelligibility of the Voice of God.

To quote further from *The Institutes* is unnecessary for our present purpose. The few extracts which we have considered capture the substance of what can be gleaned from this source. We may conservatively conclude that, whenever Calvin broaches the subject of biblical inspiration, he invariably acknowledges the cooperation of the two inseparable elements, the divine and the human. Calvin always seeks and finds an appropriate way in which to point to that cooperation without denying, diminishing, or obscuring the divine mystery of biblical inspiration. Calvin is equally sensitive to the fundamental difference between knowledge of the heart and of the mind. It must be freely conceded, of course, that, when those excerpts are divorced from their general context in *The Institutes,* they become too ambiguous in themselves to sustain a firm decision on biblical inerrancy. Consequently we now turn our attention to Calvin's biblical commentaries, hoping that they will yield more conclusive evidence.

Calvin's comments on II Timothy 3: 16 and on II Peter 1: 20 are directly relevant to our present theme of biblical inspiration. Commenting on II Timothy, he states: "First, he [Paul] commends the Scriptures on account of its authority: and, secondly, on account of the utility that springs from it. In order to uphold the authority of the Scripture, he declares that it is divinely inspired; for, if it be so, it is beyond all controversy that men ought to receive it with reverence. This is a principle which distinguishes our

religion from all others, that we know that God has spoken
to us, and are fully convinced that the prophets did not speak
at their own suggestion but that they were the organs of the
Holy Spirit to utter only those things which had been
commanded from heaven. Whoever then wishes to profit in
the Scriptures, let him, first of all, lay down this as a settled
point, that the law and the prophecies are not a doctrine
delivered by the will of man, but dictated by the Holy Spirit.
. . . Moses and the Prophets did not utter at random what
we have from their hand, but, since they spoke by divine
impulse, they confidently and fearlessly testified, as was
actually the case, that it was the mouth of the Lord that
spoke. . . . This is the first clause, that we owe to the
Scripture the same reverence which we owe to God, because
it has proceeded from him alone, and has nothing of man
mixed with it.''[47]

This often quoted contribution from Calvin is rich with
references to the nature of biblical inspiration, and for this
very reason it is particularly vulnerable to misinterpretation.
Its interesting, even tantalising, phrases stir the enthusiastic
mind. The Scripture is ''commanded from heaven'',
''divinely inspired'', spoken ''by divine impulse'', and
''dictated by the Holy Spirit''. Also, ''it was the mouth of
the Lord that spoke'' the Scripture which ''proceeded from
him alone, and has nothing of man mixed with it''. From
this concentrated association of the precise words of Calvin,
or its like, it is very tempting to conclude that Calvin can
only be referring to biblical inerrancy. But the reality of the
case is that this association selects exclusively from only one
half of the mystery of inspiration, whereas Calvin
scrupulously presents us with the whole mystery. There is
a delicate balance evident in Calvin's statements. For
instance, he talks in terms of the prophets testifying,
uttering, and speaking before he states that there is nothing
of man mixed with the Scripture. Only a person with free
will can coherently testify, utter, or speak in any meaningful
sense of these words. Thus, while Calvin makes it perfectly
clear that God spoke, he is equally emphatic that man also
spoke. With his references to the prophets as ''the organs of

the Holy Spirit'', to the law and the prophecies as ''a doctrine dictated by the Holy Spirit'', and to Moses and the prophets who ''spoke by divine impulse'', Calvin not only acknowledges the willing human participation but he underlines it almost to the point of redundancy. The balanced view of biblical inspiration which emerges from the integration of those phrases matches the thought pattern of the passages taken from *The Institutes*. Consistently, Calvin finds appropriate ways of pointing to the mysterious cooperation of the divine and the human in biblical inspiration. On the one hand, men are instrumental, as indeed are the law and the prophecies, and on the other, the Holy Spirit is active and the doctrine of Scripture is exclusively divine in origin. Far from being evasive about biblical inspiration, Calvin stresses the ministry of the Holy Spirit, the doctrine of Scripture, and the instrumentality of humankind. But the true heart of the matter is simply that God has graciously spoken to humankind.

Calvin's comments on II Peter 1: 20 recall that the prophecies are not the private suggestions of humankind but the indubitable oracles of God who speaks to us through the Scripture. Next, he tells us that ''the beginning of right knowledge is to give that credit to the holy prophets which is due to God. . . . He [the author of II Peter] says that they were moved — not that they were bereaved of mind, (as the Gentiles imagined their prophets to have been,) but because they dared not to announce anything of themselves and only obediently followed the Spirit as their leader, who ruled in their mouths as in his own sanctuary.''[48] It is evident from his remarks that Calvin believes that the mind of the prophet is quite definitely active during prophecy. First, Calvin states plainly that the prophet is not ''bereaved of mind'' as the Gentiles believed their prophets to be. Then he adds that the prophets have the Holy Spirit as their leader. A co-operative mind is required to make the decisions which are necessarily involved in obediently following a leader. In other words, the intelligent participation of the prophet was an intrinsic element in biblical prophecy. Nevertheless, the prophets were ''moved'' and the Holy Spirit ruled in the mouth of the prophet, "as in his own sanctuary". If we recall the orienting nature of cordial knowledge and the intellective quality of theological knowledge, then we can readily understand how the prophets were free to use their minds even as they obeyed humbly the Holy Spirit. The contents of this passage do not conflict with any of our previous conclusions. In fact, they seem to confirm them. Calvin's remarks both on II Peter 1: 20 and on II Timothy 3: 16 reveal his vigilant concern to acknowledge, on the one side, the ministry of the Holy Spirit and, on the other, the instrumentality of humankind. The consistency observed between the material taken from his commentaries and that selected from *The Institutes* suggests strongly that a study of further passages will consolidate our earlier findings.

Calvin refers explicitly to the currently controversial theme of dictation in the introductory remarks to his commentaries on the Gospels. Commenting on the shortest Gospel, Calvin writes: "Mark is generally supposed to have been the private friend and disciple of Peter. It is even believed that he wrote the Gospel as it was dictated to him by Peter, so that he merely performed the office of amanuensis or scribe. But on this subject we need not give ourselves much trouble, for it is of little importance to us, provided we hold that he is a properly qualified and divinely ordained witness who put down nothing except by the direction and the dictation of the Holy Spirit.''[49] Here Calvin leaves us in no doubt about his priorities. The proper qualifications of the author of Mark's Gospel are Calvin's primary concern. They have a significance for Calvin that dwarfs the importance of the true identity of the author. Historical details are interesting and worthy of comment, perhaps even instructive, but they are necessarily of secondary importance to Calvin. Matters relating to the doctrine of Scripture are always of first importance because they are not subject to the weaknesses of human approval. While there are ample critical grounds for questioning the authorship of Mark, Calvin is certain that only a "divinely ordained witness" could receive "the direction and dictation of the Holy Spirit". Moreover, his careful choice of those two phrases allows him to span the logical gap between the divine and the human as they point to the inexplicable mystery of their conjunction.

Interestingly, Calvin couples the two decisive activities of the Holy Spirit, namely "direction" and "dictation". Dictation by itself could conceivably take the form of automatic writing as an almost mindless, essentially mechanical action. But, when dictation is taken in conjunction with direction, as Calvin does, such a possibility is deliberately eliminated because only a participating mind can be directed. Moreover, according to Calvin, the Holy Spirit both guides and prompts the "ordained" Gospel writer who experiences something far more personal than detached mechanical writing. Indeed, Calvin states elsewhere that God "dictated to the four Evangelists what they should write, so that, while each had his own part assigned to him, the whole might be collected into one body".[50] Evidently Calvin believes that the dictation of the Holy Spirit is associated with the various human roles played by the individual Gospel writers. This occurs without compromising the divine plan of those Gospels. We may say that Calvin directs our attention to the fact that, although some form of verbal inspiration may seem to account for the various parts of the Scripture, the existence of the whole points ultimately beyond human words to the mystery of the "body" of Scripture. If the parts are truly a whole, then that whole is greater than the sum of its individual parts and its rationality exceeds that of its literal elements. Thus we may safely say that, while it would be very foolish to base a definite decision on those two brief quotations alone, they strengthen our suspicion that the more evidence we examine the less viable biblical inerrancy appears as an explanation of Calvin's approach to the Scriptures.

Commenting on Paul's thought in Romans 15: 4, Calvin stresses that there is nothing in Scripture that is not useful for our instruction and for the directing of our lives. He writes, "This is an interesting passage, by which we understand there is nothing vain and unprofitable contained in the oracles of God. . . . Whatever then is delivered in

Scripture we ought to strive to learn; for it would be a reproach offered to the Holy Spirit to think that he has taught us anything which it does not concern us to know; let us then know that whatever is taught us conduces to the advancement of piety.''[51] The context of this passage shows that Calvin's immediate concern is with the scope and the doctrine of Scripture, not with its precise wording. Our experience of literature in general tells us that we do not need the Holy Spirit to teach us the words of Scripture. We can memorise them without divine aid by exercising normal human gifts. Consequently, Calvin focuses attention on what we ought to learn from the Holy Spirit, namely, whatever is "delivered in Scripture" or "contained in the oracles of God", phrases which strongly echo the notion of a "depository of doctrine". In other words, we ought to learn the doctrine of Scripture. According to Calvin, our great Teacher is the Holy Spirit who takes us beyond the literal surface of Scripture into the spiritual depths of doctrine, and therefore to "the advancement of piety". The teaching of the Holy Spirit has direct practical results in our lives. Indeed, we find nothing that is personally "unprofitable". Clearly, in this passage, we cannot ignore Calvin's emphasis on the ministry of the Holy Spirit in our personal lives without drastically distorting the meaning of the passage. In any case, we assume that Calvin is not commenting here as a biblical literalist for, if he were, then he would be uncharacteristically verbose since the words "contained" and "delivered" would then be obviously redundant.

Having covered a fair amount of ground, we seem to be little further forward in our search for decisive evidence for or against the contention that Calvin is the founding father of modern biblical inerrancy. There is, on his part, an uncanny silence on this subject. Why doesn't he state in plain and simple words what he believes to be the authentic mode of biblical inspiration? Is his very silence some kind of clue for us? Perhaps this subject is not quite as straight-forward as it might first appear. From what we have learned so far, it seems that Calvin believes in an unspecified or unspecifiable form of doctrinal inspiration which is firmly grounded in the mystery that God has graciously spoken to humankind. The fact that he uses such a variety of ways in which to refer to this kind of cooperation between the divine and the human strongly suggests that he is very much aware of his own limitations as he points to what ultimately eludes human articulation. If this is actually the case, then many adherents of biblical inerrancy effectively ignore it. For they conclude rashly, on the basis of quotations like those we have already cited, that Calvin understands dictation to mean verbal, not spiritual, dictation. Although we can cite no decisive passage from his works to refute such an unwarranted conclusion, we can gainfully consider further detailed aspects of Calvin's studies.

Calvin's response to the words "by grace you have been saved" in Ephesians 2: 5 is very instructive. He explains, "I know not whether some one else inserted this, but, as there is nothing alien to the context, I freely accept it as written by Paul".[52] First, Calvin concedes willingly that he has no certainty about the origin of this phrase. Evidently Calvin has in mind the possibility that it is an addition to Scripture which occurred during transcription. Secondly, refusing to resort to any extrinsic arbitrament, Calvin appeals directly to the scriptural context as authoritative. This appeal is of course indirectly relevant to the precise wording of Scripture, but Calvin is primarily concerned with the meaning of the passage. We can say, on the one hand, that, since he is not mesmerised by the presence of a biblical enigma, he can remain open to the message of Scripture without sacrificing his critical ability.[53] On the other hand, Calvin will not pursue logical complexities at the expense of spiritual awareness. In the absence of convincing evidence to the contrary, he seems to be perfectly content to accept that this surprising phrase was "written by Paul". Calvin's response here is in complete accord with our apprehension of the natures of the two modes of persuasive knowing. On the one hand, he sees no need to annihilate his powers of human reasoning but, on the other, he recognises their limitations through his reliance on cordial knowledge.

With his comments on Hebrews 9: 1, Calvin again reveals

his keen awareness of the value of the scriptural context of a passage. As a result of his critical acumen, he is able to declare, "I think there is a mistake in the word 'tabernacle', nor do I doubt that some unlearned reader, not finding a noun for the adjective, and in his ignorance applying to the tabernacle what had been said of the covenant, unwisely added the word 'tabernacle'".[54] Here we find Calvin applying his critical knowledge in service of the doctrine of Scripture. He uses the knowledge that the meaning of a word depends on its context and that in such a context those meanings conspire against the presence of an alien word or phrase. In fact, Calvin is not particularly concerned with isolated words, although he is prepared to discuss their presence wherever they oppose or obscure the meaning of the passage.

Again, at I Timothy 1: 3, Calvin uses his critical apparatus to focus on the meaning of the passage. There he states, "Either the syntax is elliptical, or the particle *hina* is redundant; and in either case the meaning will be clear".[55] We cannot doubt Calvin's scholarship nor can we claim that he is reluctant to employ it to advantage. In this particular case, Calvin applies his knowledge to the question of the style of the passage. But he decides that, since the meaning will be clear however this question is decided, there is no need to pursue the matter further. This example demonstrates that Calvin's literary abilities are placed in the service of the "body" of Scripture. It is the meaning of Scripture that is of paramount importance to him. The precise wording only concerns him in so far as it sheds light or shadow on the meaning of the passage. This can be seen also from his comments on James 4: 7 where he writes, "Many copies have introduced here the following sentence: 'Wherefore he saith, God resisteth the proud, but giveth grace to the humble.' But in others it is not found. Erasmus suspects that it was first a note in the margin and afterwards crept into the text. It may have been so, though it is not unsuitable to the passage."[56] Rather than multiply similar quotations unnecessarily, we merely note that throughout his writings Calvin demonstrates consistently his firm conviction that the meaning of a biblical passage far outweighs its detailed wording.[57]

If Calvin were to limit himself strictly to the explicit word, that is, to the descriptive and demonstrative functions of statements and texts, he would be much more severely restricted in his approach to Scripture. In particular, if he were an exclusively critical scholar, then he would be forced to rely repeatedly on his own literary apparatus in his over-riding concern to define and to defend the verbal precision of the 'authorised' text of Scripture. Instead of appealing to the locus and the purpose of a word, phrase, or passage as guided by the Holy Spirit, Calvin would probably end up irrationally idolising a supposedly literal text. The latter would actually rely to a considerable extent on his own creative and natural knowledge of transcription, of identifiable human modes of textual corruption, of formalised elements of style *etc.* This would be necessary in order for him to provide the many required 'inerrant' analyses of biblical 'obscurities'. Our judgment is perhaps a little extreme, for there are of course numerous other factors that should be taken into account. Nevertheless, the verbal inerrantist has probably foremost in his critical mind the collection or the creation of 'relevant' information; whereas Calvin seems content to point, in so far as he is able, *through* the words, the phrases, and the passages of the Scripture to its doctrinal meaning. Calvin believes that he is guided by the Holy Spirit as he looks through the words to the Word of God whom he recognises as the true meaning of life and doctrine. In this way he by-passes a sophisticated, but superficial, essentially critical apprehension of the Scripture. He also counteracts to some extent the creation and the worship of idols by the imaginative mind. As modern literature shows, those gods so readily develop a life of their own, turn on their human creators, and impose their own conventions and applications on human literary skills.[58]

Calvin's comments on the use made by the New Testament writers of Old Testament passages shed considerable light on his own approach to the text of Scripture. Those writers did not always quote the Old

Testament passages *verbatim*. Sometimes their applications of Old Testament texts present us with difficulties. For example, with respect to Romans 10: 6 Calvin notes, "This passage is such as may not a little disturb the reader, and for two reasons. It seems to be improperly twisted by Paul and the words themselves turned to a different meaning".[59] Similarly, Calvin explains that in Romans 11: 8 Paul does not "record what we find in the prophet, but only collects from him this sentiment that they were imbued by God with the spirit of maliciousness so that they continued dull in seeing and hearing".[60] Also, Calvin maintains that, in Ephesians 4: 8, "To serve the purpose of his argument, Paul had departed not a little from the true sense of this quotation", and that "there is rather more difficulty in this clause ['and gave gifts to men']; for the words of the psalm are, 'thou hast received gifts for man', while the apostle changes this expression into 'gave gifts' and thus appears to exhibit an opposite meaning".[61] Even from those few quotations, it is obvious that Calvin does not regard Paul as a verbal inerrantist.

Although what he means by "inspiration" does not have universal application, John Murray puts his finger right on the pulse when he says of those passages that "the all-important point to be observed is that Calvin in each case goes on . . . to show that what appears to be an unwarranted change is one perfectly compatible with the designed use of the passage . . . , a use furthermore in perfect consonance with the inspiration under which the apostle wrote".[58] Calvin demonstrates ably how the use of Deuteronomy 30: 12 in Romans 10: 6 is only an apparently improper application. He also shows how "Paul penetrates to the very fountain" of Isaiah's doctrine in Romans 11: 8, and he explains how "careful examination of the psalm" reveals that Paul communicates its doctrinal theme in Ephesians 4: 8. In each case, Calvin acknowledges without hesitation or qualification the bald fact that Paul does not quote the Old Testament *verbatim*. Calvin makes a conscious effort to grasp the reason for the apostle's action. According to Calvin, the apostle exercises his rightful freedom as he chooses to

communicate only the substance of a particular Old
Testament passage to suit his immediate purpose. In other
words, Calvin is fully aware of the fact that Paul does not
regard the precise wording of Scripture as invariably
necessary to the communication of the Gospel. He realises
that Paul's pre-eminent priority is that communication and
that all of Paul's references to Scripture, whether in word or
in spirit, serve that inspired purpose. We have already
observed that Calvin's own treatment of biblical passages
makes discerning use of human reasoning. He shares with
Paul an unwavering awareness of the purpose of a passage
and a constant concern for its biblical context, neither of
which is used to annihilate human reasoning. Perhaps
Calvin is deliberately following the example set by Paul.
Granted that we still lack unequivocal evidence against the
view that Calvin is a biblical inerrantist, this possibility is
becoming more and more remote. While Calvin recognises
that biblical inspiration is ultimately a mystery, he realises
with Paul that the human words of Scripture are not
important in themselves. Paul's treatment of the words of
Scripture strongly suggests that they have an intellective
function. Because *they point beyond themselves through their context
to their substance and beyond that to Jesus Christ,* both Calvin and
Paul believe that, under the guidance of the Holy Spirit, the
human words of Scripture can be replaced by an expression
of their substance. It is the doctrine of Scripture that is of
paramount importance. All other considerations have to be
treated accordingly. Consequently, Calvin sees nothing but
consistency in Paul's thinking on those occasions when the
apostle looks through the exact wording to the doctrine of
Scripture in his communication of the Gospel.

    We now turn our attention to some passages in Calvin
that are said to cause the most acute difficulty for the verbal
inspirationalist.[62] In Matthew 27: 9 there is a reference to
Zechariah 11: 13 that is incorrectly attributed to Jeremiah.
Calvin remarks, ''How the name of Jeremiah crept in, I
confess that I do not know, nor do I anxiously concern
myself with it. The passage itself clearly shows that the name
of Jeremiah was put down by mistake for that of Zechariah,

for in Jeremiah we find nothing of this sort, nor any thing
that even approaches to it.''[63] Once again, Calvin appeals to
the context and the meaning the passage to help him to
decide on what appears to be a scribal error. Yet he is careful
to state that he is not ''anxiously'' concerned about this
error. This fits neatly into the emerging pattern of our study
of Calvin's thought but it casts no favourable light on the
feasibility of verbal inerrancy.

There are two difficulties associated with Acts 7: 14-16
which leave Calvin in no doubt about the occurrence of
errors in the Scriptures. First, there is the question of
Stephen's report of seventy-five souls accompanying Jacob
in Egypt. Secondly, there is the statement that Abraham
bought a sepulchre of the sons of Hamor rather than of
Ephron the Hittite. With regard to Acts 7: 14 Calvin
comments, ''Whereas he saith that Jacob came into Egypt
with seventy-five souls, it agreeth not with the words of
Moses; for Moses maketh mention of seventy only. . . . This
seemeth to me a thing like to be true, that the seventy
Interpreters did translate that truly which was in Moses. . . .
I think that this difference came through the error of the
writers (copyists) which wrote out the books. And it was a
matter of no such weight, for which Luke ought to have
troubled the Gentiles which were accustomed with the Greek
reading.''[64] Here Calvin suggests that an error came from
the hand of one of the copyists of the Greek Old Testament.
It was of such little consequence, however, that Luke did not
trouble the Gentiles with its correction. This suggestion
indicates that Calvin believes that Luke was prepared, albeit
in unusual circumstances, to sacrifice detailed accuracy for
the sake of uncontentious purpose, a belief which is entirely
consistent with Calvin's appreciation of Paul's writings.

Calvin's comments on Acts 7: 16 need not detain us long.
He writes, ''And whereas he saith afterward, they were laid
in the selpulchre which Abraham had bought of the sons of
Hamor, it is manifest that there is a fault [mistake] in the
word Abraham. For Abraham had bought a double cave of
Ephron the Hittite [Genesis 23: 9] to bury his wife Sarah in;
but Joseph was buried in another place, to wit, in the field

which his father Jacob had bought of the sons of Hamor
for an hundred lambs. Wherefore this place must be
amended.''[65] This error, which is obvious from the context,
arose according to Calvin in the course of transcription.
Calvin's ready acknowledgement of it indicates that he does
not regard the received text of Scripture as errorless. Indeed,
it reminds us of his reference to the neglect, error, and
audacity of humankind.[44]

Depending on the vowels supplied to the same Hebrew
consonants of one term in Hebrews 11: 21, this term can
mean either 'bed' or 'staff'. Thus the text reads that Jacob
worshipped either 'on the top of his bed' or 'on the top of his
staff'. Calvin's response to this particular difficulty seems to
assume much of what we discussed in the preceding
paragraphs. He explains, ''And we know that the apostles
were not so scrupulous in this respect, as not to
accommodate themselves to the unlearned, who had as yet
need of milk; and in this there is no danger, provided
teachers are ever brought back to the pure and original text
of Scripture. But in reality, the difference is but little; for the
main thing was that Jacob worshipped, which was the
evidence of his gratitude.''[66] Calvin states plainly here that
the writer of Hebrews was more concerned with the spiritual
nourishment of 'babes in Christ' than with his own accuracy
in a detail of this kind. Calvin himself reveals that his
attitude to the author of Hebrews matches his responses to
Paul and Luke. Calvin believes that the tolerance of an error
of insignificant detail, which does not detract from the high
purpose of the passage, is perfectly compatible with the
divine inspiration of the New Testament writer. Although, if
taken in isolation from the body of examined evidence,
Calvin's understanding of the New Testament writers
merely casts doubt on the assertion that he believes in some
form of verbal inerrancy, this understanding finds a
comfortable niche within the general environment of
Calvin's thought. Calvin appears to be following the New
Testament writers with his approach to the Scriptures.

We can present no clear-cut, decisive evidence for or
against the contention that Calvin is a biblical inerrantist.

Nevertheless, the balance of the presented evidence tilts heavily against biblical inerrancy. In fact, we can say confidently that Calvin believes that the human word of Scripture is "accompanied" by "a sure testimony" to persuade the faithful. There is a certainty of cordial knowledge and a frailty of explicit human knowledge. Yet our human words become intellective as they are oriented by the "inward persuasion of the Holy Spirit". According to Calvin, the indissoluble mystery is the intelligibility of the Voice of God. His approach to this mystery is incarnational in that he relates invariably to the different roles of the human and the divine in the one act of biblical inspiration. The Holy Spirit was pleased to work through the literary forms and skills of the original writers who plied them humbly and obediently in the service of Jesus Christ. The Spirit of God condescended to work through the linguistic milieu or context of obedient servants like Paul, Luke, or the author of Hebrews whom Calvin follows with his own approach. Personal and intelligent participation, "the ministry of men", was not compromised then, nor should it be now.[11] The spiritual nature of persuasive knowing limits critical reflection in the service of cordial knowledge which is a doctrinal knowledge of the heart. Matters of Scriptural doctrine are not subject to the weaknesses of human approval since the doctrine of Scripture is an invariant form of cordial knowledge. Thus the Scriptures are instrumental to the truth of God which employs but transcends human words. The meaning of Scripture is greater than the sum of its words. The governing tenor of Calvin's thinking derives, therefore, from his solid belief in the mysterious inscripturation of doctrine, from his vigilant awareness of the divine primacy of the purpose of Scripture, and from his unfailing fidelity to the divine authority of the doctrine of Scripture. In spite of the lack of direct evidence, we conclude that Calvin does not believe in mechanical dictation, in historical inerrancy, or in any kind of biblical literalism. In general, all supposedly comprehensive, purely critical apprehensions of the Bible are by their very nature anthropocentric and, therefore, incompatible with Calvin's Christofocal theology and with the spiritual nature of persuasive knowing.

CHAPTER 3

BIBLICAL MECHANICS

CALVIN realises that genuine difficulties often confront
the reader who wishes to embark on a theological study
of the Scriptures. In fact, he presents *The Institutes* as his
answer to the question of how to prepare for such a study.
The need for some kind of preparation is no less relevant
today. Many modern biblical commentaries seem to be
written for people with considerable critical ability and with
sophisticated biblical knowledge. Consequently, the novice
or general reader is liable to be bewildered by the multitude
of specialised concepts and detailed footnotes which appear
so often to divert his attention. Unlike the commentaries of
Calvin, many of the more recent species tend to submerge
the continuity and the meaning of the biblical text in
references to its complexities. Questions of origin,
formation, defect, transmission, and translation are, of
course, interesting but they are only important in themselves
to the critical mind. Persuasive knowing involves more than
the mind. It coordinates both cordial and intellective
knowledge. This is why Calvin regards theology as sacred.
Yet he is not alone in his reservations about the scope of
critical knowledge. When topics like literary forms or
original sources are raised, many committed Christians
respond uneasily.

Although those Christians cannot always defend their
presentiments effectively against the trained literary scholar,
they are fully persuaded that often the biblical message is
sacrificed on the profane altar of intellectualism. On matters
of detail, they feel that the immediacy of a biblical passage is
frequently strangled in order to facilitate the extraction of
remote, literary minutiae. And on larger issues, they find
themselves, sometimes surprisingly, in agreement with

D

Calvin. In a straight choice between major biblical events, like the Incarnation, the Transfiguration, the Resurrection, the Ascension and Pentecost, and the transient reasoning of the critical mind, however brilliant, they believe that they have no real option but to oppose the creations of the intellect. How could the human imagination possibly compete successfully with the divinely inspired Scriptures? Such a possibility defies faith. Although they are not as eloquent as Calvin, they do recognise that unaided human reasoning cannot even begin to apprehend the events of the Gospel. However, while Calvin no doubt sympathises with those who hold the Scriptures in the highest esteem, he never scorns the gift of human reasoning nor its instrumentality under the guidance of the Holy Spirit. As we have already observed, Calvin never isolates the doctrine of Scripture from sacred theology. Indeed, he rightly regards human reasoning as the servant of sacred theology. This means that he is opposed to all fundamentalist habits of the mind because they attempt to collapse the Scriptures onto a literalist plane of expedient apprehension. Those habits are not merely unhelpful but downright misleading. Where then can we possibly go from here? The road to philosophical liberalism is closed since it leads to the devaluation of the doctrine of Scripture and the route to pristine fundamental- ism is barred because it depreciates theology. The way forward is of course Calvin's approach to the Scriptures but, first, we take a slight detour in order to visit the modern biblical mechanic.

The modern biblical mechanic is not a rare species threatened by extinction. Countless numbers of Christians find it difficult to see the surmountable obstacles which are placed in the way of growth in wisdom before God and humankind by fundamentalist habits of mind. They assume reasonably that the reader of the Bible does not need to know much about modern theology with its sophisticated critical techniques. They claim that a straightforward under- standing of the Scriptures can be gained by anyone with a modicum of common sense. Thus even the prospective student of theology should first acquire the requisite

fundamentalist biblical knowledge before he exposes himself
to a study of those biblical commentaries which are
manifestly intensive, but questionable, elaborations of the
primary literalist material. Moreover, since the Scriptures
have their divinely pre-established harmony, and therefore
unity, the surest way for the biblical student to attain an
integrated understanding of them is by relying on a simple
literalist system. Consequently, his attempts to grasp a
coordinated apprehension of the Scriptures do not progress
far beyond his persistent efforts to extend his supposedly
literal knowledge of them. In effect, he applies what we can
justifiably call biblical mechanics. Within this framework
the biblical mechanic, or the biblical literalist, defines,
describes, and demonstrates many primary concepts and
basic statements. By regarding the biblical corpus as a
collection of God-given truths which have been cast in the
sacred literalist mould, he confines his activities, as far as
humanly possible, to what is a quasi-mechanical approach to
the biblical material. In fact, this approach has a remarkable
appeal to the modern mind because it resembles so closely
those methods of classical science which have permeated the
very fabric and framework of our supertechnological age.

Without doubt biblical mechanics has been regularly
applied with the primary and sincere aim of promoting the
understanding of God as the Father and the Creator who has
revealed himself to us in Jesus Christ. The role of the biblical
mechanic is to apply his mechanics in such a way as to aid
the Christian's understanding of events that occur in the
world by explaining them in terms of the given biblical
truths which lie unambiguously and accessibly on the
literalist surface of the Scriptures. However, it is not
recognised often enough that the key concept of the biblical
mechanic is the construction of simplified truths which are
derived from the Scriptures. Paradoxically, while the
biblical mechanic regards the latter as the unique and
comprehensive source of the unchanging and unchangeable
primary data of revelation, he actually studies his own
simplified truths. Human thinking, articulation, and
literature are, generally speaking, extremely intricate

phenomena, as the Bible amply illustrates. Thus we can say that the phenomena of human communication are much more like the motion of waves upon the surface of an expanse of water than like the movement of a steam locomotive on rails. Yet the biblical mechanic chooses to believe the complicating oversimplification that the inspired writing of the Scriptures involved intermittent suspensions of the laws of the created order by superventions of the revealing law such that the unambiguous tracks of literalist truth were laid down for all subsequent created time. Besides he simply ignores the great variety of biblical modes of communication. This alone should be sufficient to warn us of the length to which the biblical mechanic is prepared to stretch his literalism in his attempt to defend his fundamentalist habits of mind.

The choice of the motion of waves as a simile for human communication is not random. An essential ingredient of such movements is an underlying oscillatory motion. Motions of an oscillatory nature are basic to a very large number of problems in science.[67] Our chosen simile is actually typical of many physical problems in the real world. Interestingly, scientists often tackle a complex problem by isolating what they regard as the essential components of the phenomenon under investigation. This reductive approach identifies a set of simpler problems, each of which embodies an essential component of the initial complex phenomenon. The relatively easier study of individual members of that set is then undertaken. In our simile the simpler component is an oscillatory motion to remind us that students of the natural sciences often seek first in their investigations to understand a simple oscillation problem. It may seem rather strange to be discussing elementary aspects of oscillatory motion in the context of biblical literalism but the fact is that we are not far removed from the topic of biblical mechanics. What we have just been referring to as part of scientific procedure is closely related to the activity of the biblical mechanic. Just as the scientist separates out oscillatory motion as an essential component of the motion of waves on a surface of water, so the biblical mechanic singles out and, therefore inevitably, but often unwittingly, simplifies for himself what he thinks is the obvious and important aspects of a particular biblical passage. One highly significant difference exists however; the scientist simplifies intentionally whereas the biblical mechanic simplifies inadvertently.

The biblical proclamation of the Gospel in book or letter form is an extremely complex mode of communication, hence the abundance of commentaries. It is impossible for anyone to grasp the whole complex significance of an entire biblical composition at one go, even on a purely literal basis. Since the biblical mechanic has the same intellectual equipment as the rest of us, he too must begin by identifying literary forms like the parable, the miracle, or the Gospel story. Then he selects aspects of the chosen passage that are significant to him. This legitimate, reductive process enables him to study a set of simpler biblical lessons, each of which embodies an essential component of the original complex composition. In principle, the biblical mechanic tries to obtain a purely literal understanding of the Scriptures. In practice, his very attempts to adhere to the apparently literal truth rely tacitly on thought processes which defeat his good intention. By virtue of his selections from the Scriptures, the latter become for him theology-laden and his grasp of those selections is experience-loaded. Generally ignoring those circumstances, which are irredeemable in the absence of the ministry of the Holy Spirit, the biblical mechanic proceeds first to acquire, then to apply, scriptural information as if all truths could be obtained by a suitable superposition of biblical truths, there being no alternative, valid interpretations.

In order to highlight some salient features of the biblical mechanic's approach to the Scriptures, we consider a few elementary details of a concrete example from modern science. Then we run a comparative eye over a typical representation of biblical mechanics. Specifically, we examine how a student of mechanics handles the arrangement of a small heavy object fastened to the lower end of a light elastic spring. The spring is fixed at its upper end and it is free to move in a vertical line. The observed resulting motion of the object is a regular up-and-down oscillation along the vertical line of the central axis of the spring. The first step in apprehending this arrangement is to simplify the actual physical system to a more manageable arrangement.[68] Typical reductive simplifications are the following:

(i) we replace the small heavy object by a point mass having position but occupying no volume of space;

(ii) we replace the light elastic spring by a weightless spring;

(iii) we assume that the force on the particle due to gravity is constant, directed vertically downwards, and proportional to the mass of the oscillating point;

(iv) we assume that the force vertically upwards on the point mass due to the spring is given by Hooke's Law, namely, that the tension in the spring is proportional to its extension;

(v) we assume that all other forces, for example, resistances to motion due to air friction, are zero.

This set of simplifications provides us with a less complicated system comprising a single point mass acted upon by specified forces and it is more readily handled by the available mathematics.

In classical mechanics, when we have a system of particles acted on by specified forces, we use Newton's Laws of Motion to provide a system of [differential] equations which connect the accelerations of the particles [the second time derivatives of their coordinates] with the forces acting upon them. In our example, the mass of the particle times its downwards acceleration is equal to the weight of the particle less the tension in the spring. The resulting equation is the equation of simple harmonic motion. Beginning with a specific physical situation we have constructed a mathematical simplification of its motion. We can now solve this equation by standard methods using additional information about the initial conditions. The details of this procedure do not concern us here beyond our acknowledgement that those formal operations are carried out and that they lead to a solution from which predictions can be made about the motion of the simplified system. Those predictions can then be compared with the observed behaviour of the physical system and, if the agreement is good, we regard the mathematical simplification as satisfactory. If the agreement is poor, then we must re-examine our several assumptions and make more realistic ones, such as taking into account the mass of the spring or perhaps the action of resistive forces. We might even be driven to question the validity of applying Hooke's Law or Newton's Laws. The important thing is that we continue to amend our simplified system until it becomes satisfactory at the given state of scientific knowledge. In science, theoretical systems are of course only satisfactory in restricted circumstances.

Our example also illustrates for us several features which are characteristic of many scientific methods. Since those features have important correlates in Calvin's approach to theological inquiry, we mention them now in preparation for our later discussion. First, we note that our simplified system is to some extent formalised. Our satisfactory system takes the form of a mathematical simplification based on identifiable, fundamental postulates, like Hooke's Law or Newton's Laws of Motion. The development of the theory proceeds rationally from those postulates. Anything that cannot be derived from them is alien to the theory and, therefore, it is rejected. In fact, all scientific research seeks to formalise scientific theory to the greatest possible extent but only mathematics ever comes within striking distance of a fully formalised system. In general, we can say that scientific theories are formal by which we mean that they are semi-formalised. Next, we note that three different kinds of terms appear to have been used in the discussion of our simplified system. There are standard terms like 'plus', experimental terms like 'oscillation', and theoretical terms like 'simple harmonic motion', which seem to fall neatly into logical, experimental, and theoretical categories respectively. Actually, no clean-cut distinction can be drawn in science between empirical and theoretical terms for the simple reason that invariably the empirical evidence has a say in the determination of the scientific theory and *vice versa.*

Consequently, we must take those categories with a pinch of salt, as it were. Lastly, we note that our simplified system comes to us already clothed with an interpretation which is securely grounded on the given physical system. This physical system lends concrete meaning to our mathematical system. As a satisfactory first approximation, the interpretation of our mathematical system allows us to make empirical predictions which can then be physically investigated. Indeed, all scientific theories are anchored in the reality of the natural order by specific physical situations. Without that anchorage, scientific theory would soon be adrift on the tempestuous seas of capricious speculation.

It is one thing to assert that the scientist must turn his head to mathematics and his hands to experimentation. It is quite another to claim with the logical positivist that a scientific statement is meaningful if and only if it can be experimentally verified. We consider a well known counter-example of this popular theme. Newton's first Law of Motion states that 'every body perseveres in its state of rest, or of uniform motion in a straight line, except in so far as it is compelled to change that state by forces impressed on it'. The first Law of Motion is clearly unverifiable but it is certainly not meaningless, as the overwhelming success of Newtonian mechanics testifies. The continuous scientific use of fundamental postulates like this law tells us that scientists handle comfortably aspects of scientific theorising which are not reducible to scientific predictions but which none the less give rise to those very predictions. Yet an instrumentalist interpretation of modern science denies the formative function of this kind of postulate. According to the instrumentalist view, scientific theories make predictions about phenomena, phenomena provide the only meaning for scientific statements, but what underlies those phenomena does not concern the scientist. On this view, the student of mechanics predicts certain oscillations of a point mass using his mathematical system but he has no real interest in the small heavy object. For him, reality is what the theory predicts and the world of science is a world of intellectual satisfaction. Clearly, the instrumental view of science unhinges scientific theory from reality and itself from the actual practice of science.

As the student of mechanics knows from the outset, a small heavy object really does exist. In fact, its existence helps to recall the notion of a point mass that is so often used in Newtonian mechanics. While we apprehend the world on the basis of theory, theory is rooted in the world. We can say that in our simplified system the theoretical term, point mass, has a real referent in the world, that is, the small heavy object. In general, a realist interpretation of science acknowledges that behind all scientific theory lies a commitment to the reality of both the rationality and the intelligibility of the world. The scientist cannot prove that there is a real, external world to be investigated and apprehended. He simply believes it. On a realist view, the theoretical terms of scientific theory point beyond themselves to those real things from which they take their initial and all subsequent bearings. Here we are really talking of the mysterious relation between theory and reality, between the rational and the empirical. Our apprehension of reality is established, assessed, and expanded on the basis of scientific theory which, in turn, is originated, tested, and transformed on the basis of our experience of reality. As part and parcel of modern science, scientific realism arises not by philosophical reflection but out of the practice of science.

There are several things about our discussion of this simple scientific example which can assist our understanding of the activity of the biblical mechanic. Acting like the student of mechanics, the biblical mechanic undertakes, as a first step in apprehending the Scriptures, the simplification of the biblical corpus to a more manageable arrangement, although he does not acknowledge this action. His tacit assumption seems to be that the meaning of the biblical corpus is equal to the sum of the meanings of all its isolable parts. Certainly, this assumption appears to follow directly from his belief that biblical truth exhibits its own self-authenticating harmony and unity of divinely dictated human words, those words being precisely accurate in their meanings. In any case, the biblical mechanic feels free to use tacitly what can reasonably be seen as a set of reductive simplifications which resemble those presented earlier. A typical set of literalist simplifications, arranged in a sequence that parallels our scientific example, is the following:

[i] he replaces tacitly a biblical passage, like a miracle or a parable, with one having an interpretation but occupying no position within the biblical corpus;

[ii] he replaces tacitly the biblical connections with conceptual constructions that arise from hidden assumptions;

[iii] he assumes that the interpretation of the passage remains essentially unaffected;

[iv] he assumes explicitly that the meaning of a passage obeys his law of biblical literalism, that is, it is defined, described, and demonstrated comprehensively by the precisely written words;

[v] he assumes that all other aspects, for example, resistances to truth due to his spiritual blindness, are irrelevant to his declared meaning of the given passage.

This combination of assumptions, or one like it, provides the biblical mechanic with a much simpler system comprising an isolated section of the Scriptures supposedly containing a specified literal meaning. Such a combination can be handled readily by expedient modes of apprehension. But more to the point, there are obvious grounds for calling the biblical literalist a biblical mechanic, although the scientist may justifiably complain of the possibility of guilt by association. Having acknowledged that the scientist strives always to make his assumptions explicit, it is clear that we are not pointing the finger at him. Yet a zeal to condemn the biblical mechanic is inadvisable for his activities can be fruitfully regarded as scientific procedure in embryo. In the light of our comparison, it is less surprising to learn that many Christians who are science graduates display a strong literalist or fundamentalist streak.

Besides, mathematical simplifications based on Newton's Laws of Motion are deterministic in the sense that the coordinates [and therefore the velocities, the accelerations, *etc.,*] are in principle precisely predicted from analytical expressions provided with the necessary and sufficient initial information. Also, the construction of Newtonian simplifications for mechanical systems has carried modern science an impressive distance along the path of understanding. It is only when the scientist tries to develop Newtonian simplifications for mechanical systems that are very large, very small, or in extremely rapid motion, that his efforts produce unacceptably poor results. Newton's Laws of Motion seem to yield adequate simplifications for most of the objects of our everyday world in which the velocities and the dimensions of things are so familiar. On the very large scale, we meet the problems of cosmology and, on the very small scale, we encounter those associated with molecules, atoms, and elementary particles. Many of those extremely large or small objects move with very high velocities, sometimes approaching the ultimate value of the speed of light. In those circumstances, Newton's Laws of Motion, even for objects of familiar dimensions, require modification according to Einstein's theories of relativity. We can say that, in general, Newton's Laws of Motion can be applied on an everyday size-scale to mechanical systems with a reasonable expectation that they will provide an adequate simplified system.

Hence, the science graduate who is a student of the Scriptures is attracted, at least initially, to biblical mechanics because the latter appears to provide a parallel, deterministic, analytical approach to the Word of God. Apparently, its literalism defines, describes, and demonstrates Christian truth in terms of the primary given data of revelation. Like Newtonian mechanics, biblical mechanics can also carry the earnest seeker of literalist truth a very long way. In the process, it can build such confidence in itself that its followers eventually lose sight of its initial assumptions or else they resent all references to its hidden presuppositions. Since forgotten or hidden assumptions are not by nature open to question, they are given free reign to exercise undue authority. In other words, biblical mechanics can generate a stultifying complacency, one which blinds its proponents to the anthropocentric nature of its basic assumptions.

Our outline of biblical mechanics illustrates several features that are characteristic of many approaches to the Scriptures. First, we note that our literalist scheme is formalisable only in a loose sense. Nevertheless, it does have recognisable postulates from which sensible deductions can be made. For example, it follows from the first simplification that a miracle or a parable has a message in its own right. Thus we can say that the development of biblical mechanics may, but does not always, proceed rationally from those postulates or their like. Anything that conflicts with them is unacceptable to the theory and, therefore, it is excluded. In fact, all study of the Scriptures seeks to formalise knowledge to the greatest possible extent but the resulting formalisations can never hope to match those of mathematics, or even those of modern science. In general, we can say that systematic studies of the Scriptures are formal by which we mean that they are semi-formalised. Next, we note that three different kinds of terms have apparently been used in our discussion of the representative literalist scheme. There are neutral terms like 'and', scriptural terms like 'miracle', and theoretical terms like 'literalism', which seem to slot nicely into logical, biblical, and theological categories respectively. Actually, there is no acid test that distinguishes between biblical and theological terms. Invariably the biblical content has some say in the formulation of theology and theology makes its presence felt in the translative coinage of the biblical treasury. This is obviously a very serious problem for all forms of literalism. Consequently, the use of those categories is not plain sailing. Lastly, we note that the literalist scheme comes to us supposedly clothed with an unique literalist interpretation which is equivalent to the given biblical corpus. This revealed corpus gives tangible meaning to biblical mechanics. As a committed approach to the study of the Scriptures, the literalist interpretation provides a biblical apprehension that can be subjected to the rigours of

Christian experience but it does not automatically follow that it will be subjected to those rigours. Indeed, all genuine approaches to the study of the Bible produce interpretations which must stand on the bed-rock of Christian experience. Without that secure foundation, biblical study would soon be wandering aimlessly in the densest wasteland of intellectualism.

To claim that the committed Christian should put his mind to biblical study and his life to Christian experience is one thing but to assert with the biblical mechanic that the Bible should be understood literally is to raise an entirely different issue. Exactly what do we understand by the directive that the Bible is to be understood literally? Does the Bible literally give such a directive? As it does not, can we not then conclude that biblical literalism has condemned itself by its own theory of meaning? Besides, the very use of fundamental postulates, whether tacit or explicit, tells us that biblical students operate effectively on a theological basis which is not fully reducible to either biblical or experiential terms. None the less this basis lends meaning to Christian experience, despite the fact that the literalist interpretation denies the formative function of this kind of postulate. According to biblical mechanics, biblical study gives rise to equivalent statements about the biblical content; the biblical content provides the only meaning for theological statements; but what underlies that content does not concern the biblical mechanic. Indeed, he believes that it does not even exist. On the fundamentalist view, the biblical mechanic relates to his Christian experience in terms of his literalist system of biblical knowledge but he has no real interest in anything beyond that knowledge. For him, reality is what biblical literalism creates and the world of biblical mechanics is a world of intellectual satisfaction. Clearly, biblical literalism decouples itself from the actualities of Christian living, that is, from the reality of our lives in Christ.

At this point we recall that Calvin presents *The Institutes* as a suitable form of preparation and instruction of candidates in sacred theology for the reading of the divine Word.[1]

According to Calvin, students in sacred theology should be prepared and instructed before they proceed to study the Scriptures. He recognises that Christ is the reality to which all Scripture points and that, from the outset, we should come to the Scripture with a foreknowledge of theology that is sacred, not profane. In fact, Calvin tells us that our experience of Christ allows us to relate to the biblical material. While we should apprehend the reality of Christ in our lives on the basis of our study of the Scriptures, our approach to the Scriptures should be firmly grounded in our experience in Christ. On Calvin's view of biblical interpretation, a theological term has a real referent in Christ. In general, a realist interpretation of the Scriptures acknowledges that behind all genuine biblical study lies a commitment to the reality who is the Word and who gives us the Holy Spirit. The biblical student cannot prove that there is a living God who reveals himself in Christ. He simply believes it. On a realist view, both theological and biblical terms point beyond themselves through the Holy Spirit to those real things of Christ from which they derive meaning. Here we are really talking of the mysterious relation between the human and the divine, between word and Word, and between theology and reality. Our apprehension of God and of self is established, apprehended, and transformed on the basis of biblically enlightened theology which, in turn, is originated, tested, and transfigured on the basis of our experience in Christ. Theological realism results not from philosophical reflection but out of the practice of Christian devotion.

We mentioned earlier that biblical mechanics has the built-in means to blind its proponents to the anthropocentric nature of its basic [tacit or explicit] assumptions. The power of those means to entrench fundamentalist modes of thought should be neither underestimated nor misunderstood, however, especially in the privileged century which witnessed the graceful abdication of Newtonian science.[69] Apart from a relatively few scientists, hardly anyone at the end of the last century envisaged a profound transformation of the very foundations of modern science which then appeared to be solidly established upon a preponderantly Newtonian basis. Today, of course, we are all wise after the events. Most of us have learned the valuable lesson that Newtonian science at its best presupposed its own eventual demise and at its worst seems to have worked for its self-preservation. Einstein has taught us that even the development of the most important and apparently most verified science proves to be completely unpredictable.[70] His outstanding scientific contributions have clearly shown us that the special and general theories of relativity are the natural consequences and outgrowths of all the scientific research that has been carried out since the days of Newton and even of Galileo. Although Einstein's theories changed unexpectedly and drastically some very prominent concepts, we can now appreciate with the benefit of hindsight that the concepts which suffered such transformations were actually the less significant ones. The really important basic concepts remain as integral parts of the new theories.

Isn't there a valuable corresponding lesson to be learned by the biblical mechanic? Shouldn't biblical mechanics at its best presuppose its own eventual demise? Unfortunately, biblical mechanics at its worst seems to work for its own self-preservation. But we have just referred to some of the weaknesses which lurk in its effective assumptions. And, earlier while discussing our scientific example, we noted the need to re-examine our several assumptions when the agreement is poor between the predictions of our simplified Newtonian system and the observations of the given physical system. More realistic assumptions often require to be made, such as taking into account some other aspects of reality like the mass of the spring. Perhaps it may even be necessary to go as far as to question the universal validity of some well-established laws like Newton's Laws of Motion. Likewise in biblical studies, the sincere scholar should surely be prepared to reconsider previously neglected factors when his simplified system does not match the actualities of Christian living. For example, the biblical mechanic predicts that God created in six days the very world which convincingly denies this in so many scientific ways. Here we have for many people a profound conflict between biblical literalism and Christian experience. Also, since there is no literalist endorsement of literalism in the Bible, the biblical mechanic should be prepared to re-examine the comprehensive applicability of his man-made law of biblical literalism. After all, if scientists in the pursuit of truth were willing to challenge Newton's theory of gravitation by testing, checking, and cross-checking it throughout well over two hundred years,[71] then shouldn't the biblical mechanic in following Jesus Christ be prepared to do as much, if not more, in order to challenge his own conceptual constructions of the biblical content?

Yet the great reluctance of the biblical mechanic to re-examine his hidden or forgotten assumptions is not without historical parallel. For instance, modern science should probably have been more prepared than it was for the demise of Newtonian mechanics. Nineteenth century mathematics had received a poignant reminder of the fallibility of long-established conceptual systems when Euclidean geometry was successfully challenged as the universal description of real space. Besides, a profound lesson on the meaning of geometric words and concepts was also associated with the momentous events which surrounded this challenge. In fact, the recollection of certain elementary aspects of this episode in the development of modern science are particularly rewarding for the biblical student who seeks a deeper appreciation of the theology of Calvin. But we must start at the beginning. Around 300 B.C. Euclid compiled and systematised the current knowledge of plane and solid geometry in his famous *Elements*. This work began from seemingly simple definitions, axioms, and postulates and it built up a vast system of results, each of which depended only on previous results. Although his work represented the birth of mathematical rigour,[72] Euclid's definitions shared a common weakness. Euclid believed that the points and the lines of his geometry were in fact the points and the lines of the real world. So he saw no reason to attempt to distinguish with sufficient clarity his geometric definitions from the common notions of point, straight line, circle, *etc*. This meant that the student of Euclidean geometry was free to make his own intuitive associations with the basic definitions which therefore served as essentially heuristic devices.[73] Curiously, the basic information contained in those definitions plays no formal part in the development of the Euclidean edifice. The axioms and the postulates are far more important. Both classes of proposition are simply asserted to be valid and from them the whole system is deduced using purely logical inference. No additional non-logical operations are permissible in the formal development which makes no clear distinction between axioms and postulates. Actually, this is not strictly true for Euclid himself made tacit assumptions. [The biblical mechanic is in good company!] For example, Euclid used the common knowledge that in a plane a given straight line which passes through the centre of a circle intersects that circle exactly twice. Yet this knowledge is not deducible from the axioms or the postulates. Nevertheless, those occasional lapses do not detract appreciably from the astounding logical power of the great Euclidean synthesis.

The axioms of the Euclidean system deal essentially with general notions whose significance obviously transcends their immediate geometric relevance. For example, the first axiom tells us that things equal to the same thing are equal to each other. The postulates are quite different. They deal with specifically geometric matters. For instance, the first postulate states that two points determine a straight line. The foundations of Euclidean geometry are represented by only five axioms and five postulates which display remarkable simplicity and obviousness with one exception.[74] Nine of the fundamental propositions are attractively terse and intuitively obvious but the fifth postulate is uncharacteristically long and relatively complex. [It says: If a straight line falling across two straight lines makes the sum of the interior angles on the same side less than two right angles, then the two straight lines intersect, if sufficiently extended, on that side.] The latter sticks out like a sore thumb. In fact, Euclid himself was never entirely satisfied with this wordy and obscure postulate. Nevertheless, the great Euclidean synthesis presented humankind with a vast systematisation of geometric knowledge that appeared to epitomise scientific completeness and certainty.

Over the many centuries since Euclid, there have been innumerable unsuccessful attempts to derive by logic alone the fifth postulate from the other nine self-evidently valid, fundamental propositions. The great ambition which motivated those efforts was to demonstrate that the validity of the fifth postulate really rested on the undisputed validity of the nine. Girolamo Saccheri adopted a rather unusual approach to this problem.[75] His strategy was to use the opposite of the fifth postulate, to reinterpret the second postulate, and to identify the resulting contradiction. [Actually, he denied an equivalent of the fifth postulate, the parallel postulate, which says: Given any straight line, and a point not on it, there exists one, and only one, straight line which passes through that point and never intersects the first line, no matter how far they are extended. The second straight line is said to be parallel to the first one.] Since no mathematical system can tolerate a contradiction, the invalidity of his new fifth postulate would be demonstrated by one. Without troubling ourselves with unnecessary details, we note simply that Saccheri set out on what proved to be a very long road which tried his undoubted patience and his great skill. Eventually he encountered a proposition that conflicted with his notion of the straight line. He regarded this proposition as the desired contradiction and he published his work under the revealing title *Euclid Freed of Every Flaw*. The industrious Saccheri was never to know the full measure of his own admirable achievement. He had unwittingly discovered what was recognised ninety years later as non-Euclidean geometry. In 1823, a remarkable coincidence occurred in the world of mathematics. The Russian Nikolay Lobachevski and the Hungarian Johann Bolyai, working independently, discovered simultaneously non-Euclidean geometry.[75] What interests us greatly as biblical scholars is that the key to the new geometries lay in divesting the mind of preconceived notions of a straight line.

The secret is to let the propositions of the particular geometry under investigation determine the nature of a straight line. Had Saccheri recognised the profound significance of his labours, no doubt his book would have had a very different title!

As things turned out, the various discoverers found different kinds of non-Euclidean geometries by indirectly denying the fifth postulate through changing the parallel postulate. If we claim that there is no such second line [The No Parallel Postulate], then we end up with elliptical geometry, whereas if we assert that at least two such lines exist [The Many Parallels Postulate], then we produce hyperbolic geometry. The concrete realisation is that, although the Euclidean system applies obviously within the ecological niche of humankind, the alternative non-Euclidean geometries may be needed to inform us of the real worlds of the very large and of the very small. This is a clarion call to physical reality to establish the domains of validity of the various geometries. Here the biblical student receives a sharp reminder of the inescapable need to look beyond his conceptual systems to the reality of God in Jesus Christ. Equally striking is the recognition that the geometric propositions of the specific system determined the geometric meanings of point, line, *etc*. In fact, rather than define those special words, a semi-formal version of a particular geometry allows the totality of propositions in which they appear to provide their implicit definitions. The biblical mechanic should note that even in semi-formalised geometric systems the meaning of a word or a concept is determined by its holistic role. In general, the sharpness of notions like definition, description, and demonstration seems to lose their cutting edges as logical rigour increases, taxing the limitations of purely critical reflection.

From our little excursion into the development of modern mathematics we learn that the definition of a geometric word or concept is not as straightforward as it first appears. Even with the relative rigour of semi-formal geometric systems, the undefined meanings of terms like point and straight line are determined by the totality of propositions in which they occur. Those terms depend on the meaning of the theorems in which they figure. At this point, Calvin's concern with the context of a passage and with the intellective nature of theological words leap immediately to mind. We recall that, according to Calvin, there is a certainty of cordial knowledge and a frailty of explicit knowledge and that our human words are intellective, being oriented by the "inward persuasion of the Holy Spirit". Thus, if human reasoning is not compromised in persuasive knowing, the undefined meaning of theological and biblical words depend on the totality of statements in which they appear. Those words and concepts depend on the meaning of the passages in which they figure. This means that the meaning of Scripture is greater than the sum of its words, a thought that does not perplex Calvin for he believes that the human word of Scripture is "accompanied" by "a sure testimony" to persuade the faithful. But we have just acknowledged that the various geometries also have to be accompanied by an empirical testimony to convince the scientist, not of their logic, but of their meaningfulness. Moreover, Calvin tells us plainly that, using human reasoning alone, we are incapable of progressing beyond "foolish" thoughts and "absurd" words on studying the Scriptures.[3] And as if to push Calvin's point home, modern mathematics establishes for us that the basic terms of a geometric system remain empty of meaning until an interpretation is found. Mathematical systems are grounded in reality in order to give them physical meaning, whereas theological systems are spiritually meaningful only when grounded in the reality of God and of self. While those purely mathematical systems are neither foolish nor absurd, any theological analogue would be by virtue of its isolation from the reality of Jesus Christ. Thus, the findings of modern mathematical studies show the great power of Calvin's insight that all theological systems which depend exclusively on critical reflection, including biblical mechanics, lead to foolishness and absurdity. They also help to reveal the wisdom of Calvin's persistent concern for the context and purpose of the given passage as opposed to individual words. We can say that there is nothing intrinsically wrong with the isolation of a parable or a miracle as a first step in apprehension. But that first step should be closely followed by a second step which directs us away from our preferred reliance on human reason and routine. By taking into account the context of a passage, the second step helps to ensure that our critical knowledge is less destructively limiting for it throws more weight upon the action of unknown or unrecognised agencies.

What we learn from mathematics suggests that by the word context we should understand all biblical knowledge that has a direct bearing on the meaning and the purpose of a given passage. Thus the context includes, in ever widening waves of awareness, the adjacent pericopes, the immediate theme, the Gospel or Epistolary emphases, and the doctrinal and biblical congruities. If this could be achieved in a satis-factory way, then many of the problems arising from the literalist simplifications [i] and [iii] would be avoidable. But the problems associated with simplifications [ii], [iv], and [v] would then be greatly intensified. The nub of the matter is the sheer physical impossibility of purely critical reflection to cope with the immensity of the biblical material and to make all the relevant connections. But this is not a real dilemma for Calvin who recognises that we need the Holy Spirit to transform the dead letter of Scripture into the living Word of God.[47] Only the Holy Spirit can lead us to the appropriate biblical connections as we seek to find Jesus Christ through the Scriptures. Unlike the mathematician, the biblical student looks through the system, not at it. Through the ministry of the Holy Spirit, the biblical passage retains for us personally its authentic biblical context. By addressing itself to the experience of the follower of Jesus Christ, including his resistances to the truth, that is, his preconceptions, preferences, and predicaments, the biblical passage becomes personal but not subjective. The spiritual message or meaning is both divinely inspired and humanly accommodating. As such it deals directly with theology-laden biblical content and biblically loaded theology. Clearly this approach to the Scriptures represents a severe challenge to the law of biblical literalism. It departs markedly from a rigorously literalist understanding of the Bible as it highlights the limitations of critical reflection. Since it seems to follow from what we already know of Calvin's work, we now consider further aspects of his approach to the apprehension of the Scriptures.

CHAPTER 4

PERSUASIVE APPREHENSION

TO regard the biblical contents as a source of exclusively
definitive, descriptive, and demonstrative knowledge is
to attribute to them the primary purpose of conveying purely
explicit knowledge. According to Polanyi, the only logical
thing that we can do with this kind of information is to reflect
critically on it.[76] There is, of course, always a risk involved
in working with any normal literary corpus: namely, that the
translated and transmitted text can be doubted because it
may contain mistakes acquired throughout the history of its
handling. This is where critical reflection comes into its own.
Polanyi emphasises that "the peculiar risk that we take in
relying on any explicitly formulated knowledge is matched
by an opportunity offered by that explicit knowledge for
reflecting critically on it".[76] In other words, we can check
the information contained in such a received text. For
example, we can compare it with other sources which are
strongly attested by similar comparisons or we can run
internal checks on the received text. Indeed, we have already
had occasion to note that Calvin is prepared to run such
checks and, whenever possible, to benefit from their
results.[64,65] We recall that Calvin does not advocate the
suspension of the powers of human reason on reading the
Scriptures but rather their openness to the guidance of the
Holy Spirit. For Calvin, there is no separation of faith and
reason.

Critical examination of any literary source is possible for
two reasons: first, because the text is a thing external to us
and not something we shape ourselves, and secondly,
because even though it is an object external to us, it can
communicate to us. A text presents us with something to
which we can attend. In reading and studying it, we are, so

to speak, playing back to ourselves something that we have read before in order to attend to it in a critical manner. Of course, as Calvin knows only too well, a critical process of this kind may go on for its own sake and, with a text as comprehensive as the Bible, it may even last a life-time. Indeed, some Old Testament and New Testament scholars have spent so much time engaged in the exclusively critical examination of the Bible, book by book, pericope by pericope, sentence by sentence, or word by word, that they no longer regard it as anything other than the book of the ancient Hebrew and Christian religions. Supposedly pure critical reflection has blinded so many scholars for whom the Scriptures have become merely a representative corpus. Unlike Calvin, they seem to have rejected the insight that the use of human reason alone is a very fallible way of reading the words and, therefore, of hearing the Word of God.

Calvin is firmly convinced that a proper understanding of the Scriptures demands more than merely critical reflection. According to him, the Bible is not just another piece of outstanding literature. It requires a different approach and so he prescribes a persuasive apprehension of the Scriptures. He reminds us that the Gospel has an intrinsically persuasive power: "the apostle rightly contends that the faith of the Corinthians was founded 'upon God's power, not upon human wisdom' [I Corinthians 2: 5] because his own preaching among them commended itself 'not in persuasive words of human wisdom but in demonstration of the Spirit and of might' [I Corinthians 2: 4]. For truth is cleared of all doubt when, not sustained by external props, it serves as its own support."[77] Calvin believes in the personally persuasive knowledge of God through the Word of God. The finest human wisdom cannot possibly imbue the most eloquent words with a convincing power that can ever compare with heavenly doctrine clothed in the humblest words. There is an objective knowledge of God that is gained through the power of God in the personal experience of his presence. Here we have a reminder that Calvin never forgets his own profoundly personal experience as a young man whom God humbled to teachableness and enlivened to new studies of the Holy Scriptures.[78] This experience has a lasting effect on him. It is small wonder then that we find him emphasising, not logical demonstration or accurate description, but rather the simple need to allow the persuasive power of the truth to become personally effective in human lives. For Calvin, the problem of how to persuade people finds its answer in the simplicity of the self-evident and self-authenticating Word of God. Calvin is thoroughly convinced that we can only know God and self truly through the persuasive power of Scripture, a power that "is clear from the fact that of human writings, however artfully polished, there is none capable of affecting us at all comparably. Read Demosthenes or Cicero; read Plato, Aristotle, and others of that tribe. They will, I admit, allure you, move you, enrapture you in wonderful measure. But betake yourself from them to this sacred reading. Then, in spite of yourself, so deeply will it affect you, so penetrate your heart, so fix itself in your very marrow, that, compared with its deep impression, such vigour as the orators and philosophers have will nearly vanish. Consequently, it is easy to see that the Sacred Scriptures, which so far surpass all gifts and graces of human endeavour, breathe something divine."[77]

Calvin learned from Renaissance humanism of the value of logic and of philosophy, of the arts of speaking and writing, and of the great importance of law and of history. Yet none of them can offer anything that compares with the persuasive power of the Scriptures. In spite of its frequently "rude and unrefined style",[79] its unique power penetrates not only the mind but also the heart through the work of the Holy Spirit. Thus the teachings of the Bible, "crammed with thoughts that could not be humanly conceived",[77] have a God-breathed dimension which involves knowledge of a divine origin. This spiritual dimension of knowledge escapes all purely critical approaches to theology with their stress on logical methods and on explicit statements. Calvin resolves to return, therefore, to the sources of the faith where "the truth cries out openly that these men [the biblical writers], who, previously contemptible among common folk, suddenly began so gloriously to discourse of heavenly mysteries, must have been instructed by the Spirit''.[80] Two things are particularly worth noting here for they are recurrent themes. First, Calvin indicates that persuasion is the work of the Holy Spirit. Secondly, his belief in this power as personal has a solid biblical basis. In general, from his many and varied references to a knowledge of the heart, to what we call cordial knowledge, we can confidently conclude that Calvin believes firmly in the personal and objective persuasiveness of the Word of God.

The Holy Spirit persuades us that the Scriptures ''flowed to us from the very mouth of God by the ministry of men''.[11] In itself Scripture is a dead and ineffectual thing just like any other historical document.[81] Therefore, when Calvin says that ''Scripture exhibits fully as clear evidence of its own truth as . . . sweet and bitter things do of their taste'',[82] the evidence of which he speaks is not like the evidence we have of the physical world around us. It is evidence of divine reality, which is self-evident and self-authenticating. On the one hand, this kind of evidence is objective and independent of us. Coming from beyond us, it can only be known in accordance with its own divine nature. There is nothing that we can think or do that will equip us to discover, to receive, or to appreciate such evidence. On the contrary, people can only respond to the divine persuasion that the Scriptures are the School of the Holy Spirit through the work of the same Spirit, for Calvin states plainly that ''the testimony of the Holy Spirit is more excellent than all reason''.[12] On the other hand, this kind of evidence becomes personal and enlivening for us as we surrender our inadequate, inhibitive interpretations and our restrictive, logical routines.

Bridging the infinite gulf between our apprehension and the divine reality of God as the Father and the Creator of humankind is Jesus Christ who confronts us with the truth in the Holy Spirit. The Spirit of Christ ''must penetrate our hearts to persuade us that they [the prophets] faithfully proclaimed what had been divinely commanded''.[12] Clearly, it would be not only irrational but sheer folly for the

Christian to ask for some authority higher than the Holy Spirit. In persuasive knowledge we are dealing with something more than mere intellectual assent. The whole person is involved. Personal participation is required if we are to be grounded on the objective reality of God himself. By the grace of God, this grounding edifies our persons and it transforms our prior apprehension of the truth of God. For the action of the Holy Spirit opens the way for the loving reaction of the person who is simultaneously prompted and equipped to respond obediently to the Spirit's revealing and transforming acts.

Uncompromisingly, Calvin writes, "Scripture will ultimately suffice for a saving knowledge of God only when its certainty is founded upon the inward persuasion of the Holy Spirit".[17] We reach a transforming knowledge of God only under the persuasion of his truth upon our persons. The initial movement is from God to humankind and without it there cannot be saving knowledge. Calvin, therefore, ascribes consistently little importance to other kinds of knowledge as evidence in support of the authority of the Scriptures. Perhaps surprisingly, Calvin ranks alongside those external varieties of knowledge an explicit knowledge of the contents of Scripture, including a detailed knowledge of its different literary styles, of its complex originalities, and even of the various miracles of Scripture. Since all true knowledge of God arises from our loving obedience to the inward persuasion of the Spirit on reading the Bible, we can say with Calvin that it is "not right to subject it to proof and reasoning", and that "we seek no proofs, no marks of genuineness upon which our judgment may lean: but we subject our judgment and wit to it as to a thing far beyond guesswork"![11]

Those and many other statements of Calvin leave us in no doubt about the unique nature of a persuasive apprehension of Scripture. It brings a certainty which surpasses human reasoning without dispensing with that reasoning. Persuasive knowing does not rely on human proof. In fact, it subordinates or coordinates critical reflection. Saving knowledge of God can banish all idols from the mind by liberating us continually from the bondage of our entrenched preconceptions, our conservative prejudgments, and our habitual preoccupations. While human reasoning, proof, and judgment are not abandoned, these "human testimonies"[77] are in themselves insufficient or even vain but they have a necessary, subservient role in the persuasive plan of things. Indeed, in direct reference to those activities, Calvin advocates that "in the reading of Scripture we ought ceaselessly to endeavour to seek out and meditate upon these things which make for edification".[83] Granted the right priorities, human reasoning, judgment, and proof can "make for edification". What we ought really to guard jealously against is wild guesswork and rash speculation. All our critical efforts should be guided by the Holy Spirit. They should concentrate on, and limit themselves to, matters that relate obediently and humbly to the meaning and purpose of the passage of Scripture as inspired by the Spirit. We can draw considerable consolation from Calvin's dictum that "the true meaning of the Scripture is the natural and simple one",[84] although the critical mind will probably want definitions of "natural" and "simple".

Earlier, we noted Calvin's persistent concern for the context and the purpose of a given passage, a concern that has surprising echoes in the world of modern mathematics. We can now point out without fear of prejudice that Calvin actually states that "there are many statements in Scripture the meaning of which depends on their context".[85] Incidentally, for those who wish to study this matter in greater depth, fine extended examples of Calvin's contextual approach are his discussions in *The Institutes* of the Lord's Supper[86] and the Ten Commandments.[87] His contextual approach springs from his Christofocal theology which is well served by tools adapted from Renaissance humanism. Calvin avoids the two obvious temptations to distort atomistic analyses of biblical knowledge into sheer relativism or arbitrary positivism. His studies testify strongly that, in the right hands, those tools can serve a persuasive apprehension of the meaning of a passage or a text. If biblical studies are to be authentic, that is, if they are to yield transforming knowledge of God, then they must deal with knowledge that points beyond itself to Jesus Christ. Calvin defends staunchly his firm conviction that only a persuasive apprehension of the Scriptures will edify the seeker of truth. In his own words, "God is known truly and firmly only in Christ",[88] and we receive Christ "as he is offered by the Father, namely, clothed with his Gospel".[19] Here we have stated plainly the one true purpose and the uniquely real meaning of the Gospel, to which all other considerations must direct us. On studying the Scriptures, Calvin seeks above all else the divine intention revealed in the passage and so the words that he offered on one occasion are equally applicable to all: "Here, however, we shall never attain the truth unless we fix our eyes upon Christ's intention and give heed to what he is driving at in that passage".[89]

Somehow we must learn to look through the passage of Scripture to Christ himself. But since we cannot investigate the living Word using human reason alone, the only way in which this can be accomplished is under the guidance of the Holy Spirit. The Spirit of God makes the words of Scripture translucent for us. So Calvin naturally likens the Scriptures to a pair of spectacles: "Just as old or bleary-eyed men and those with weak vision, if you thrust before them a most beautiful volume, even if they recognise it to be some sort of writing, yet can scarcely construe two words, but with the aid of spectacles will begin to read distinctly; so Scripture, gathering up the otherwise confused knowledge of God in our minds, having dispersed our dullness, clearly shows us the true God".[90] Those words make it plain that Calvin understands that the persuasive unity of our knowledge of God results from the harmony of heavenly doctrine and the intellectively arranged, mean and lowly words of human language. In the presence of the Spirit, the Scriptures become a spiritual instrument which orders our previously confused knowledge of God. In other words, biblical books, passages, statements, and words all point beyond themselves to Christ. They all serve consociately his high intention. Therefore, on the one hand, our findings match those of the modern mathematician in that the individual word serves its sentence, the particular sentence serves its passage, the specific passage serves its book, the special book serves the Bible. But, on the other hand, our findings are always grounded on our persuasive knowledge that the words of Scripture serve the Word of God. Uniquely, the enlivening meaning and the saving purpose of Christ integrate the form and the content of all biblical statements. Those statements, therefore, are not confined to the recognised consistencies of the human mind. They are inherently practical, explicitly intellective, and persuasively coherent. Coessentially, this persuasive unity directs our critical faculties in the detection of errors which arise from human negligence, frailty, and audacity.

Scripture is God's answer to the human need for a true knowledge of God and of self. God in his divine wisdom has chosen it as the means to bring persons to the knowledge of salvation. It is not a hitching post but a signpost. As Winston Churchill could well have said, we should not use Scripture as a drunk man uses a lamp-post, that is, more for support than for enlightenment. Scripture is a guide for the Christian life. According to Calvin, its persuasive unity, which "could not be humanly conceived",[77] can only be apprehended, never fully comprehended. Its origin, purpose, and end coincide and transpire in the Person of Jesus Christ. In this glorious unity, "the sublime mysteries of the Kingdom of heaven came to be expressed largely in mean and lowly words".[77] Yet, this same unity is "manifestly too powerful to need the art of words", and too majestic to be "adorned with more shining eloquence".[77] Nevertheless, as we have already acknowledged, "the gifts and graces of human endeavour"[77] still find their rightful place in biblical studies.

The aim of the humanist legal scholar of Calvin's day was to discover the intent of ancient law codes in their original historical contexts. In sound biblical fashion, Calvin adapts their methods to meet theological requirements. He attempts to understand as fully as possible the biblical milieu in which a passage of Scripture resides. He realises that the study of both biblical history and its various customs can significantly colour the meaning of a text. Indeed, he could not fail to do so with his detailed knowledge of how humanist studies of the history and of the social customs of ancient Rome gave a direct understanding of the intentions and the meanings of legal texts. But the inspired intent of the biblical writer must never be given second place to any human expertise in biblical customs, history, etymology, *etc.* So Calvin advises us "not to speak, or guess, or even to seek to know, concerning obscure matters, anything except what has been imparted to us by God's Word".[83] For him, possible outlines of the original historical background, of the pristine geographical setting, or of the cultural context, of the distinctive literary forms relevant to a given passage are only useful so long as they remain intellective. As soon as they begin to eclipse the persuasive truth of the Gospel, they become dangerous idols of the human mind and they feed a fascination which fosters either religious relativism or fanatic positivism.

Calvin's thoughts on the apprehension of the Scriptures have a distinctly modern flavour. Indeed, they harmonise remarkably well with some of the most important and exciting findings of modern mathematics. We made reference earlier to the highly significant nineteenth-century discovery that there were different, equally valid, geometries. In fact, the very notion of a geometry had to be generalised to mean a theory of the properties of implicitly defined points and lines. Besides, the virtually simultaneous discovery of non-Euclidean geometry by several mathematicians challenged Euclid's right to the geometric throne. Even more significantly, it also questioned the ability of mathematics to reign over the real world. Could one single reality have a spectrum of types of points and a variety of kinds of lines? What did this pluralism imply about human reasoning?

As we have previously mentioned, Euclid first systematised geometry and so paved the way for its subsequent development. But he did much more than that. By providing a systematised geometry he demonstrated very powerfully that human reasoning is at least partially expressible in semiformal propositions. Euclid raised in a deeply impressive way the question of the formalisation of the processes of human reasoning. Consequently, it was only natural that, when Euclidean geometry was at last seriously rivalled, interest in the formalisation of human reasoning would be rekindled. In fact, the English logicians, George Boole and Augustus De Morgan, added rich fuel to this fire but coals also came from classical mathematical seams. About one hundred years ago, when Georg Cantor produced his elegant theory of sets, a bundle of set-theoretical paradoxes saw the light of mathematical day.[91] Those paradoxes shared the mysterious property of self-reference. While the original simple liar paradox of the Cretan Epimenides shows this property, "All Cretans are liars", its following expanded version[92] makes the problematic nature of self-reference abundantly clear:

The following sentence is false.

The preceding sentence is true.

When they are used separately, these two sentences make perfectly good sense but, when they are taken together, their combination is neither true nor false and a paradox remains. By referring to each other, they combine to form a loop of inter-dependence that conflicts with their individual meanings. A number of set-theoretical, self-referencing paradoxes were quickly discovered in mathematical set-theory. Together they posed the fundamental question: Can a rigorous theory of sets be formulated which closely matches our intuitive notions of a set but which also excludes the offending paradoxes? We recall that in geometry difficulties appeared as soon as an attempt was made to formalise human reasoning. Exactly the same thing occurred with set-theory. On trying to match intuitive notions with rigorous formulations or axiomatisations, paradoxes were uncovered in set-theory.

Bertrand Russell and Alfred North Whitehead responded to this situation with their now-famous *Principia Mathematica*.[92] This work attempts to eliminate the strange paradoxes from logic, set-theory, and number theory. But it has several disquieting features. Its theory of types introduces an artificial hierarchy of types of sets together with an arbitrary method of disowning certain kinds of sets. Its drastic remedy for paradoxes is virtual annihilation through total elimination of self-reference. Also, it is not immediately apparent that its methods are thoroughly comprehensive or that they are even self-consistent. Nevertheless, this contribution helped to create a great interest in the axiomatisation of human reasoning. In the general air of mathematical expectancy that characterised the first three decades of this century, doubts even arose about number theory as mathematicians entertained the real possibility that undetected paradoxes could be lying in waiting for the placid student of whole numbers. It was quite generally acknowledged that the urgent need was for an universally acceptable, consistent, complete formalisation of the modes of mathematical reasoning. But had the *Principia Mathematica* actually done what it set out to do? Had it met adequately this need?

In 1931 Kurt Gödel published a paper that revealed the incompleteness of the *Principia Mathematica* and, indeed, of all consistent axiomatic formulations of number theory.[93] He also showed that the consistency of a system like the *Principia Mathematica* could not be proved using only the methods within that system. The mysterious thing is that, if an internal proof of consistency can be found for a system, then according to Gödel's work the system itself is inconsistent. How did Gödel arrive at his mystifying but far-reaching results? His initial intention was to use mathematical reasoning to investigate mathematical reasoning. But that takes us right back to self-reference, the very thing that Russell and Whitehead took such pains to exclude. Our expanded version of the Epimenides paradox with its two inter-referential statements about statements, illustrates how easy it is to talk about language using language. But how do you talk about mathematics using mathematics? Specifically, the mathematical statements of number theory are about the properties of whole numbers. Obviously neither whole numbers nor their properties are statements. So a statement of number theory is no more than that. It is certainly not a statement about a statement of number theory. Gödel had to discover how to make mathematical statements about statements of number theory.

Gödel had the brilliant insight that, if numbers could represent statements, then a statement of number theory could be about a statement of number theory.[94] Consequently, at the centre of his work stands a code in which numbers represent symbols and sequences of symbols. This code allows statements of number theory to be understood on two different levels. On one level, they are ordinary statements of number theory, but on the other level, they are statements about statements of number theory. Having worked out his scheme, Gödel then tackled the difficult business of finding out how to transplant successfully the Epimenides paradox into a number-theoretical formalism.[94] What he ended up with was a rigorous mathematical version of the sentence: "This statement of number theory does not have any proof in the system under investigation." As we have already noted, Epimenides presented us with a paradox because his statement was neither true nor false. But Gödel generated a statement that is valid but unprovable within the given system. In fact, his work leads to the staggering general conclusion that there are valid statements of any axiomatic system which its methods of proof are too weak to demonstrate. In other words, Gödel discovered that for any axiomatic system provability is a weaker notion that validity.[95] His work also showed that the complexity of the whole numbers could not be represented by any axiomatisation.

But what has Gödel's Incompleteness Theorem got to do with the theology of Calvin? Certainly, both men found different ways of arriving at the same conclusion, namely, that provability is a weaker notion than validity. A fuller answer to this question, however, accommodates the paradox that, while this important theorem leads us to a limitative statement, Gödel's discovery forecasts a prosperous future for axiomatics. Gödel's work highlights the constant need for further studies. Since, for any consistent axiomatic system, there are valid statements which cannot be proved within the system, all such systems are incomplete. But if a system is incomplete, then it will be open to the addition of new axioms or rules. Any new system resulting from such an addition will be consistent and incomplete, just like its predecessor. Thus we can expect that in mathematics ever more powerful axiomatisations will follow endlessly. Even the formal systems of number theory promise to reward the continuing endeavours of the mathematician. In short, it seems that the mathematician's work will never be done, a happy prospect for the future of mathematics.

Obviously, it would be a great mistake to think that what has been rigorously worked out in mathematical logic should hold without modification in a completely different discipline like theology. Nevertheless, we still learn enough from Gödel's work to advance two rather interesting comments on biblical interpretation. First, if a consistent literalist interpretation of the Bible is even remotely possible, then according to Gödel's findings, either such an interpretation will be incomplete or else it will defy the formal rules of human reasoning. But if it is incomplete, it is also open to additions and, therefore, it does not qualify as a genuinely literalist interpretation. Alternatively, if it defies human reasoning, it is by its very nature something other than what is commonly understood as a consistent literalist interpretation. In others words, Gödel's Theorem suggests that, if the Scriptures are to be regarded as a system based on ordinary human reasoning, then that system cannot be a consistent, complete literalist interpretation of the Bible in any normal sense of these words. This suggestion is, of course, in full agreement with our earlier observations on the nature of the implicitly defined concepts of a semiformal geometric system. We conclude therefore that there can be no such thing as a consistent literalist interpretation of the Bible.

Secondly, for any consistent axiomatic system, there are two kinds of knowledge; knowledge that can be proved within the system and knowledge whose validity cannot be established within the system. But this is remarkably similar to the way in which Calvin deals with our apprehension of the Scriptures. As we have already discovered, Calvin talks consistently of knowledge of the heart and of the mind; what we call cordial knowledge and intellective knowledge, respectively. According to Calvin, the validity of our cordial knowledge derives solely from Christ himself through the ministry of the Holy Spirit. It comes from outside the written word which is the consistent instrument or system of the Word of God. This instrument is, therefore, incomplete in itself for God is his own interpreter. Without the guidance of the Holy Spirit, we rely on human reasoning alone which, in the form of Gödel's Theorem, tells us that any purely human formalisation of the Scriptures will be at best either incomplete and consistent or else complete and inconsistent. Both possibilities are equally unacceptable to the biblical scholar who believes that the canon of Scripture is closed and consistent. But this dilemma, which arises from the supposedly exclusive use of human reasoning, merely confirms what Calvin says: if we try to use human reason alone, then we end up with foolish thoughts and absurd words about the Scriptures. Thus with the assistance of Gödel's work we can begin to appreciate the depth of Calvin's wisdom as he concentrates not on the words of Scripture but on the doctrine of Scripture. Only the rationality of the Word through the intelligibility of the Holy Spirit can lift us beyond the incomplete or inconsistent theological systems which we build so readily out of our limited critical knowledge of the Scriptures.

In order to simplify this discussion we now introduce the notion of an isomorphism. Our usage of this word is derived from a much more precise concept in mathematics. For us, this word indicates a correspondence involving two or more structures which can be mapped onto each other in such a way that to each part of one structure there is a corresponding part in the other structure or structures. By corresponding parts we mean two or more parts which play similar roles in their respective structures. For example, in the parable of the prodigal son we have the three structures of the family in the story, the family of God, and the family of the reader of the story. These three structures are isomorphic in the sense that there can be a son, a father, a brother, a meal, a departing, a home-coming, *etc.*, which can have corresponding roles within each of the three families. Of course, isomorphisms come in all shapes and sizes and so it is not always clear when we have actually perceived one. Our necessary vagueness about the usage of this word, however, does not affect the outcome of our lowly efforts.

The perception of an isomorphism between two recognisable structures is a transforming step in knowledge for it brings meaning to the perceiving mind. In our example, if the experiences of the prodigal son, of his brother, and of his father are regarded not merely as the details of a story but rather as heuristic probes for improving our understanding of the behaviour of our own family, then we can raise a whole crop of new problems very rapidly. What we perceive is an isomorphic connection of the parable with the everyday reality of our family life. This correspondence between the two structures is commonly known as an interpretation. It is, in fact, only the lower level of what we call our biblical isomorphism. On a higher level, there is the correspondence between the family of God and the family in the story. This correspondence is the isomorphic connection with the divine reality. But we must note carefully that this higher level correspondence is never fully expressible in words. Indeed, we can only use words intellectively to point to this higher level of rationality for we can never adequately describe, define, or demonstrate what we know of God, our heavenly Father, of Jesus Christ, the Son of God, of Holy Communion, and so on. Of these precious things we are given a cordial knowledge, and so with Polanyi we can follow the thought of Calvin by saying that "we know more than we can tell"[26] and we tell more than we know.[96]

Yet the power of this divine knowledge becomes evident through our explicit interpretation of the lower level of the biblical isomorphism. For instance, it is our cordial knowledge of the Fatherhood of God that equips us for all that the true fatherhood of man can be. Our explicit knowledge of the fatherhood of man is a personal apprehension oriented by, and grounded on, our cordial knowledge of God and of self. In other words, the lower level correspondence is not perceived independently of our cordial knowledge of God. Thus in persuasive knowing there are two levels of correspondence; the upper inexpressible level involving an isomorphism between the Fatherhood of God and the fatherhood in the story and the lower explicit level involving the fatherhood in the story and our experience of fatherhood. This is why Calvin constantly refers to the correspondence between Scriptural doctrine and biblical statements when he discusses the meaning of a particular passage. As we stated earlier, Calvin's thoughts on the meaning of the Scriptures have a distinctly modern flavour. Once again, he seems to have anticipated modern thinking by finding his own unique way of handling this two-tiered correspondence which is characteristic of what we call biblical isomorphisms.

We can now draw a very important distinction between two types of interpretation for the parable. First, there is a purely speculative kind of interpretation, one under which we fail to know persuasively any isomorphic connection between Scriptural doctrine and the biblical statements. This means that the isomorphic link between the divine and the human has been severed and, therefore, that we are entirely at the mercy of our own speculative devices, in which case there is nothing, for instance, to stop us talking of a selfish father who spoiled one son and took the other too much for granted. Interpretations like this one abound. However, they have very little theological meaningfulness; under such an interpretation, theological statements do not ring true, *e.g.,* God the Father is neither selfish nor indulgent. The other kind of interpretation is theologically meaningful. Under such an interpretation, theological and biblical statements correspond. An isomorphism exists between the theology and some aspect of the Scriptures which echoes the doctrine of the Scriptures. That is why it is important to distinguish between interpretations and meanings. We can interpret the parable in terms of any human father for all human fathers act selfishly at one time or another. It is only when we take the father to be God the Father that our human interpretation is raised to the meaning of salvation for humankind.

Obviously we have only scratched the surface of this exciting topic but at least we have indicated how an appropriate approach to the study of the Scriptures, namely, Calvin's approach, can bring us transforming knowledge of God and of self. We have also shown that Calvin is thoroughly modern in his thinking. In preparation for the continuation of our study of Calvin's work, we now underscore one aspect of the personal nature of our knowledge of God and of self. It is not just the mathematician or the scientist who constructs a system for himself. The theologian, the musician, the painter, the butcher, the baker, and the candle-stick maker also do it. In fact, we can say without fear of contradiction that every human being tends to work inside an acquired system and the more successful that system is, the harder it is to reach outside in order to think about what it is doing, or more accurately to think about what we are doing with it. This is no less true of the Christian. Every Christian has a system of beliefs, his theology, which is more or less systematised. But, even if he manages by his own efforts to step outside his theological system to take a critical look at what he is doing with it, he will still be unable to advance his persuasive knowledge of God or of self. The most that he can ever achieve by merely human ability is a more eloquent, more ordered expression of his preferred system. The works of Calvin and Gödel teach us the same lesson in their own impressively different ways: critical knowledge cannot create new transforming knowledge. Moreover, according to Calvin, only persuasive knowledge can lift us out of our limited human theological systems into an enlivening knowledge of God and of self.

CHAPTER 5

PERSONAL PARTICIPATION

IN order to deepen our appreciation of persuasive knowing
as an experience involving the complete, personal
participation of the individual, we turn to Calvin's
apprehension of the image of God in humankind.[97] By the
word "image" we take Calvin to mean a reflection in some
sense like the image of an object in a mirror.[98] Calvin is
careful to inform us that God first made himself known to
created humanity as the Creator and that it was after the
Fall that God made himself known to humankind as the
Redeemer. He reminds us that the image of God that was in
created man before the Fall is restored to man in Christ.[99] In
the light of our earlier findings on his Christofocal theology,
it seems singularly appropriate that we try to look with
Calvin through the biblical account of Adam to Christ for
instruction on this crucial topic. Surely there can be no
better way to start than with Calvin's concise declaration
that "the integrity with which Adam was endowed is
expressed by this word [imago], when he had full possession
of right understanding, when he had his affections kept
within the bounds of reason, all his senses tempered in right
order, and he truly referred his excellence to exceptional
gifts bestowed upon him by his Maker".[97]

We learn from Calvin that a "right understanding"
requires more than the control of the affections and the
ordering of the senses. Indeed, according to him, the proper
coordination of the psychological and physical actions of the
person can only be secured by a right responsiveness to God
by that person. In our relations with God the Creator, our
complete beings are necessarily involved. God the Creator
holds us in being. In him we live and move and have our
being. Yet only the person who depends utterly on a

relational knowledge of God can be a fully integrated individual. We are reminded once again of the remarkable consistency of Calvin's thought as we recall the opening remarks of *The Institutes* which deal with the notion of the inseparability of our knowledge of God and of self. Nothing less than total personal participation is required in our responses to God the Creator. Moreover, if Calvin is correct in saying that Adam "truly referred his excellence to exceptional gifts bestowed upon him by his Maker", then we can say that created man had an intellective knowledge of "his excellence" which relied on "exceptional gifts" involving a cordial knowledge of "his Maker". Or, in Calvin's own vivid words, Adam had the light of mind and the uprightness of heart,[98] by which we understand that Adam had explicit, intellective knowledge of God and inexpressible, cordial knowledge of God, both of which result from a right relationship with God the Creator. We assume, therefore, that what Calvin means by a "right understanding" is what we refer to as persuasive knowing which involves, by its very nature, our complete, personal participation.

Since Calvin makes extensive use of the mirror metaphor throughout his writings, we must tread carefully in order to catch its special application to humankind. At the universal level, he tells us that the whole of creation is like a mirror in which the glory of God is reflected.[100] On the biological level, he says that its creatures are like mirrors to the wisdom, justice, goodness, and power of God.[101] But those observations do not strike us as particularly surprising or original, coming as they do from a brilliant scholar with an enlightened humanist background. Calvin could hardly fail to recognise that man lies on the boundary of the natural and the divine. On the one hand, he is created a small piece of nature and, on the other, he is created nothing less than an unique image of God. So what, for Calvin, singularly qualifies created man as made in the image of God? If Calvin effectively refers to man as a microcosm of a macrocosm or as a species within the animal kingdom, his references are only to man's natural gifts which can certainly mirror the glory of God like the rest of the known creation. Yet, as we have already noted, even an individual with an abundance of natural gifts is not in the image of God unless that person is persuaded of the divine origin and applicability of his gifts. If the natural gifts of man are coordinated and oriented by a "right understanding", however, then they are integral to the image of God in man. It is in the latter sense that Calvin can say without fear of contradiction that man's dominion over nature,[98] the upright posture of his body,[97] the inner good of his soul,[98] and in fact all that sets him apart from the rest of God's creation are tokens of the divine image. In keeping with his Christofocal theology, Calvin does not try to provide us with a precise definition of the image of God in man simply because he apprehends that image to be one of the Creator at work through the uniqueness of man. Since God is Reality, the image of Reality derives its true meaning from Reality. But we cannot circumscribe the nature of God and so it is foolish to attempt to define the image of God in man, that is, to try to define created man. Incidentally, if the image of God is restored in fallen man in Christ, then the notion of redeemed humankind as the rightful exploiter and authorised manipulator of the created order runs contrary to the insight that God the Creator is at work through the uniqueness of humankind. The cordial and intellective knowing of the student of the Scriptures requires his humble, obedient response to God the Father who is none other than God the Creator and the Sustainer of the created order. Persuasive knowledge of God and of self fosters a cooperative reverence toward that order.

Avoiding precise definitions, Calvin points out that created man is "characterised by faith, love of God and neighbour, desire and application to live in righteousness and holiness".[102] God has given the human being a body and a soul with which he can discover and enjoy the created order rather than exploit and manipulate it. With his body and soul, he is capable of establishing and developing an appropriate livelihood and he is free to express and to extend himself. Those are the natural gifts of humankind. But, according to Calvin, God has also endowed human beings with other gifts, with "exceptional gifts", and it is only through the proper application of the latter that the former can fulfil their real function. Through the eyes of faith, in the heart of love, and with a true desire to be in a right relation to God, investigation of the created order becomes participation in it. Also, the means of survival can be transformed into the riches of unselfish living and modes of self-expression can become open channels of divine love and wisdom. Thus the image of God in man consists not in the fact that man has reason and will but rather in the reality that these faculties are directed by a "right understanding" toward a loving obedience to God. Evidently, in Calvin's view, the soul and the body of man function together like a mirror in which the image of God is reflected.

Created man towers above the rest of the known creation because he alone can faithfully reflect God's glory in both word and action. Uniquely within our galaxy, humankind can knowingly image God's glory in thought and in deed. We can say that a "right understanding" carries man to the zenith of the mute, unknowing, known creation by enabling him to praise God from whom all blessings flow. And this remains true even if there are other superior forms of intelligent life at large within the unknown creation. Disruption of this right relation between the person and God, that is, wilful disobedience by the individual, is for Calvin nothing short of depersonalising. It results in the disintegration of the mysterious unity of his body and soul and in the disconcertment of his thought and action. The individual's personal equilibrium of soul, mind, and body is destroyed, as it were, in the absence of persuasive knowing. But how can we be sure that we are not putting words into Calvin's mouth? Can we provide further evidence to support what seems to be a rather strange assertion? In fact, Calvin comes to our aid here with his understanding of the concept of sin.[103] He explains that the forbidden fruit represents a test of humankind's obedience. Bearing in mind that primeval man's exercise of faith was a reliance on persuasive knowledge, we observe that, although Calvin has several

words for the root cause of sin, he strongly favours the word
"unfaithfulness".[103] By this particular word he means
essentially 'not open to the Word of God'. For him, the root
cause of sin was therefore not man's intemperance or his
pride but rather his rejection of the Word of God. In our
terms, the root cause of sin was man's rejection of the
persuasive truth of God. Created man sinned with his
refusal to hear, to accept, and to obey the Word of God.
Only "as a result, men, having cast off fear of God, threw
themselves wherever lust carried them".[103] This means that
man's rational nature was first deprived of a right
orientation and coordination and only in consequence did he
know bondage to carnal desire. As always, Calvin goes
straight to the heart of the matter: 'Unfaithfulness, then,
was the root of the Fall. But thereafter ambition and pride,
together with ungratefulness, arose, because Adam by
seeking more than was granted him shamefully spurned
God's great bounty, which had been lavished upon him. To
have been made in the likeness of God seemed a small
matter to a son of earth unless he also attained equality with
God.''[103]

If Calvin leads us to understand that Adam's original
state was one in which he had a "right understanding",
then we also appreciate that his fallen state is one in which he
has a 'wrong understanding'. Thus Calvin believes that at
the Fall man's affections were unleashed, that his senses
were disordered, and that his excellence disappeared. A
'wrong understanding' resulted as the image of God in man
and the relationship of man to God were annihilated. The
Fall fragments man's very being which reacts by striving for
its own integration and by seeking its own glory. Thus
denial of the Word of God thwarts man's real purpose,
disrupts his integrated person, and severs his right relations
with God and man. We can say that without the exercise of
true faith, without a complete reliance on persuasive
knowledge of God and of self, man is bereft of the
"excellence" of his "exceptional gifts". He has put himself
at the mercy of the devices of his disordered senses and of his
uncontrolled affections. But, by the grace of God, all hope is

not gone. As Calvin gladly reminds us, "the door to salvation is opened to us when we receive the Gospel today with our ears".[103] Cordial and intellective knowing are the spiritual dynamics of the real person in Christ.

It may appear that Calvin is placing an extraordinarily large burden on the faith of the person. In fact, he is only making explicit the inescapable and fundamental role that faith already plays in all our lives. Calvin's emphasis on faith receives strong support from what seem to be the most unlikely sources. Both the modern mathematician and the practising scientist are ultimately prepared to base their investigations on faith. Moreover, they do it for the most part without even batting an eyelid. A simple arithmetic illustration allows us to grasp the essential point. How much is eleven times eleven? We all know that it is one hundred and twenty-one. But how many of us have actually taken the trouble to draw a square with sides eleven centimetres long, next to divide it into little squares with sides one centimetre long, and finally to count those little squares? Probably very few of us because most of us would regard this exercise as quite unnecessary. Instead, we would automatically write down the number eleven and place a second eleven directly below it before drawing a line. Next, we would write down a third eleven below the line and directly under the second eleven. The fourth eleven we would place below the third one but this time displaced one space to the left and under it we would then draw a second line. Finally, we would write below the second line the number one hundred and twenty-one. The resulting multiplication sum would represent our 'proof' that, if we counted those little squares, we would be sure to find one hundred and twenty-one of them.

Obviously the method of constructing and counting squares would demand much more time and effort than the symbolic process of arithmetic multiplication requires. Indeed, the larger the numbers become the more pronounced are the practical difficulties of constructing and counting squares. Inevitably, a stage would soon be reached where, with large numbers of squares, the demands made on the person by those difficulties would outrun his concentration span and even his physical endurance, to say nothing of the limits of his material resources. Under those conditions, we would become less and less confident that he would obtain the right answer. So when we think about it, we see that we have no real choice. We must rely on the manipulation of digits according to the established simple rules of arithmetic which are assumed to hold for all numbers. But this assumption is not verifiable in all cases because the number of cases is infinite. The plain truth is that we take this assumption for granted; we believe it just as firmly as we believe that the same sun which sets today will rise again tomorrow. In general we have a firm faith in the symbolic processes of arithmetic. In particular, the mathematician by vocation schools his faith in symbolic processes with his exploration of new systems.[104] Similarly, the scientist educates his faith in the laws of nature with the experiments which he devises.[105] Although Einstein has modern science mainly in mind, his wise comments also cover our simple arithmetic illustration: "It is the aim of science to establish general rules which determine the reciprocal connection of objects and events in time and space. For these rules, or laws of nature, absolutely general validity is required — not proven. It is mainly a program, and faith in the possibility of its accomplishment in principle is only founded on partial successes."[106]

Consequently, Calvin's recognition of the central role of faith in Christian living strikes a note of empathy in modern scientific ears. Besides, the notion that our intellective knowledge of the Bible is developed as the Holy Spirit establishes and increases our cordial knowledge of Christ is sometimes faintly echoed as scientists speak of their scientific experience. Since few scientists would challenge Einstein's right to speak from scientific experience, we attend to some of his words. First, we recall that Einstein recognises freely that science has its limitations. He points out that science "can teach us nothing beyond how facts are related to, and conditioned by, each other. The aspiration toward such objective knowledge belongs to the highest of which man is capable. . . . Objective knowledge provides us with the powerful instruments for the achievement of certain ends, but the ultimate goal itself and the longing to reach it must come from another source.''[107] Here we find Einstein claiming on the one hand that science deals with objective, factual knowledge and on the other that science is not self-sufficient, depending as it does on the external motivation of scientists. This brilliant scientist is firmly convinced that commitment to the scientific enterprise has roots that run much deeper than explicit, objective, scientific knowledge.[108] Einstein believes that there is something beyond normal, explicit, scientific knowledge which not only enlivens the scientist but also enlightens him. So he talks in terms of intuition. According to Einstein, the intuition of the scientist is fed by a growing sympathy with the natural order.[109] Rephrasing Einstein's thoughts and echoing Calvin's theology, we can say that our scientific knowledge of the universe is developed as the *intuendum* establishes and increases our sympathetic knowledge of reality. In other words, we can perceive a deep isomorphism between Calvin's approach to the Scriptures and Einstein's apprehension of modern science. While Calvin's approach can be apprehended in terms of Jesus Christ, the Holy Spirit, the Scriptures, and persuasive knowledge, that is, cordial and intellective knowledge, Einstein's apprehension can be understood in terms of physical reality, a mysterious intuitive relation, natural phenomena, and sympathetic knowledge, that is, intuitive and scientific knowledge. Yet this isomorphism also highlights a significant difference between modern science and Calvin's approach. At the heart of modern science lies a fundamental faith in the rationality and intelligibility of the real universe but scientists acknowledge that the dynamics of scientific faith lie outside the domain of science. The backbone of Calvin's approach to the Scriptures is a saving faith in the Word of God and the ministry of the Spirit of God, and he seeks to unfold the biblical dynamics of faith for the biblical student. Nevertheless, we find in Einstein's thoughts on science an intriguing echo of Calvin's trinitarian theology.

Following Einstein, Polanyi discusses in considerable

depth the creative role of non-empirical powers of scientific thought. Those modes of knowing physical reality are vitally at work in all forms of scientific inquiry but they are not always acknowledged by graduates of science through fear of adverse positivistic reaction. An excellent case in point is the various distorted accounts of Einstein's discovery of Special Relativity. Those accounts have appeared in standard scientific textbooks for decades. Since Polanyi's rendering of this story shows how personal powers transcending sensory perception are essential to scientific research,[110] it captures the spirit of Einstein's thinking. So we retrace rapidly the salient features of Polanyi's version, indicating their relevance to Calvin's work. In the heyday of logical positivism, it was generally believed that Einstein developed Special Relativity[111] in order to account for the results of the Michelson-Morley experiment.[112] Those results led to the conclusion that the speed of light measured by a terrestrial observer was the same irrespective of the direction taken by the emitted light signal. On the basis of the currently accepted Newtonian theory of space, those results were anomalous. This theory predicted that the observer would catch up to some extent with the light signals sent out in the direction of the earth's motion. The speed of the light signal was expected to be slower if travelling in the same direction as the earth but faster if travelling in the opposite direction. A. A. Michelson and E. W. Morley detected no significant difference in the speed of light which could be meaningfully attributed to terrestrial motion. Within the acceptable limits of experimental error, they had shown that the speed of light was a constant.

Positivist textbook presentations of the events surrounding Einstein's discovery of Special Relativity commonly cast the work of Michelson and Morley in the principal role of crucial experiment. Those accounts portrayed this work as decisively demonstrating the need for a new theory of the relative motion of bodies. They argued that, in direct response to the observed facts and in line with the positivist description of modern scientific procedures, Einstein devised a new summary of scientific experience known as Special

Relativity. But as Polanyi and others realised, the actual sequence of events exposes the limitations of a positivist approach to scientific discovery and it highlights the personal participation of the scientist. Also, the true sequence shows the realism of Einstein's comments on the roles of faith and intuition in scientific inquiry. In his *Autobiographical Notes*,[113] Einstein traces his thoughts on relativity back to a paradox that he first encountered at the age of sixteen. According to him, and who could know better, Special Relativity grew out of his recurrent reflections on this paradox. Science is the attempt at the posterior reconstruction of existence by the process of conceptualisation. As he recalls his early experience, the substance of his thoughts at that time were: "If I pursue a beam of light with the velocity c [the velocity of light in a vacuum], I should observe such a beam of light as a spatially oscillatory electromagnetic field at rest. However, there seems to be no such thing. . . . From the very beginning it appeared to me intuitively clear that, judged from the standpoint of such an observer, everything would have to happen according to the same laws for an observer who, relative to the earth, was at rest."[113] Since with those words Einstein puts on record that intuiton was the penultimate source of his remarkable theory, he strikes a mortal blow against positivist notions of modern science. In general, he rejects the thesis that a scientific theory is merely a summary of scientific experience and, in particular, he dissociates himself from all positivist accounts of the discovery of Special Relativity. Indeed, when he was questioned directly about the part played by the Michelson-Morley experiment, Einstein stated plainly that "the Michelson-Morley experiment had no role in the foundation of the theory" and that "the theory of relativity was not founded to explain its outcome at all".[114] Einstein's personal intuition coupled to his great tenacity and fuelled by his firm faith in the rationality of nature carried his recurrent reflections to the ultimate destination of Special Relativity. In short, the personal participation of the scientist franked Einstein's intuitive and reflective treatment of this paradox, his self-

G

denying commitment, and his realist faith in the natural order. It reminds us a little of how the personal participation of the theologian is the hallmark of Calvin's cordial and intellective handling of biblical inspiration, of his self-denying commitment, and of his realist faith in Jesus Christ.

Two other related events also expose the positivist fallacy of viewing modern science as solely founded on neutral observations. Einstein acknowledges that, in his earlier years as a scientist, he had been greatly influenced by Ernst Mach's book *Die Mechanik*. Einstein recognises his intellectual debt to Mach who had criticised Newton's concepts of space and absolute rest on the grounds that they could not be tested by experiment. Mach was the father of logical positivism who conceived of science as purely grounded on sensory observations. By the way, our interest in Mach is not entirely scientific. His views on science made him a distant cousin of the biblical mechanic who conceives of theology as purely grounded on literalist observations of the Scriptures. Because Newton's fundamental concepts or postulates could not be tested by experience, Mach condemned Newton's theory as meaningless. Needless to say, he provided his own notion of meaning. According to Mach, a postulate has meaning if and only if it can be empirically verified. But as Polanyi points out, if Einstein had rejected a meaningless theory, he would not have increased and improved our scientific knowledge. In fact, Einstein established that Newton's concept of space is not meaningless but invalid, and so he proved that Mach was wrong in his condemnation of Newton's theory.

We have here another example of the stupefying power with which our conceptual constructions can engulf us. Newton's theory of space, like Euclid's nine postulates, matches our immediate sensory experiences. In our everyday world, we regard the earth as stationary and we watch the sun traverse the sky. The curious thing is that Mach, the founder of logical positivism, managed to emulate the great Copernicus. Somehow Mach had the vision to look beyond the apparently compelling evidence of his senses and to challenge Newton's unique point of absolute rest. Polanyi exposes for us this particular paradox which "lay precisely in that appeal to rationality which Mach wished to eliminate from the foundations of science. . . . Thus Mach prefigured the great theoretic vision of Einstein, sensing its inherent rationality, even while trying to exorcise the very capacity of the human mind by which he gained this insight."[115] So we have a new twist to our tale. On the one hand, Mach had the scientific insight to anticipate in important respects the work of Einstein. On the other, he was so preoccupied with his philosophical views that he did not take into account his faith in the rationality of nature, the result being that he did not fully appreciate the soundness of his intuition. Einstein, however, was the grateful beneficiary. We can say in Gödelian style that Mach made some valid statements about scientific theory that did not have any proof within the system of logical positivism. Those statements should have carried him beyond his philosophical system but they did not. We can state in Polanyian fashion that Mach told more than he knew and that he knew more than he could tell. Also, we can assert in the Einsteinian way that Mach's longing to reach the ultimate goal was not sufficiently strong. And we can say in Calvin's terms that Mach was unable to keep his affections for logical positivism within the bounds of reason or his senses tempered in right order. The plain facts are that Mach's actions could not match Einstein's intuitive and reflective handling of a profound paradox, his self-denying commitment to science, or his realist faith in the natural order simply because logical positivism rendered his personal participation captively subjective. But Mach's reactions are not unparalleled. Many literalist and liberalist scholars are found making some valid statements that do not have any justification within biblical literalism or liberalism. Those statements should carry their makers beyond their philosophical systems but they do not. Yet those scholars know more than they can tell and they tell more than they know. Their longing to reach the ultimate goal of the Scriptures is not sufficiently strong. They are unable to keep their affections for literalism or liberalism within the bounds of reason or their senses tempered in right order. Their actions do not match Calvin's cordial and intellective handling of biblical inspiration, his self-denying commitment to the Word of God, and his realist faith in God the Creator and the Redeemer, simply because biblical literalism or liberalism renders their personal participation captively subjective.

Years later, the Michelson-Morley experiment was at the centre of another interesting episode. Investigations, principally by D. C. Miller,[116] gave results that should have rightfully challenged the work of Michelson and Morley as providing valid support for Special Relativity. Miller detected an experimentally significant effect due to the terrestrial motion of the observer. When he reported his findings to the American Physical Society in 1925, however, his results were given the cold shoulder by that august assembly. Special Relativity had gained such wide acclaim that Miller's experimental evidence was swept aside in the hope that, given enough time, someone would prove it false. That assembly of scientists preferred to question the validity of hard experimental evidence rather than to abandon a comparatively new theory which none the less had already uncovered new dimensions of the rationality and intelligibility of nature. When presented with the choice of the empirical evidence or the theoretical achievement, those scientists opted to venture in faith. They placed their trust in the new disclosures of the rationality of nature rather than in the limited results of a few experiments. But events of this kind hold few surprises for working scientists who soon learn from their own personal participation "that any critical verification of a scientific statement requires the same powers for recognising rationality in nature as does the process of scientific discovery, even though it exercises these at a lower level".[24] The working scientist knows only too well that scientific reflection must be enlightened by scientific intuition if it is to be raised above the critical level, that is, above the mere improvement of scientific reasoning, to the exhilarating heights of greater scientific rationality.

We can learn, then, from the words and the actions of

Mach, Einstein, Polanyi, and a host of other renowned scientists, that the creative coordination of the psychological and physical actions of the scientist can be firmly secured only by the right responsiveness of the person to the rationality of nature. This scientific responsiveness entails positive personal reactions to challenging, intuitive insights, self-denying commitment to the scientific enterprise in the specific form of the research at hand, and a realist faith in the rationality of natural order. The whole person of the scientist is somehow involved in his relations with that rationality. The scientist is a small part of nature and, therefore, a tiny subject within modern science. Only the scientist who depends utterly on a relational knowledge of reality can hope to gain the necessary intuitive insight that will project him progressively deeper into universal rationality through scientific theory. In fact, learning from Einstein and Polanyi, we venture to suggest that the scientist has an intellective knowledge of reality which is his communicable grasp of scientific theory and which relies on an intuitive knowledge of the rationality of nature. We conclude therefore that, since sympathetic scientific knowing seems to require the complete personal participation of the scientist, the theology of Calvin has much to say to the modern heart and mind in the pursuit of truth.

As in science, so in theology critical reflection can improve the consistency, and the uses, of our reasoning. But only persuasive knowing can secure, transform, and expand our knowing. Persuasive knowledge is a knowledge of Christ which is active knowledge involving the offence, or the challenge, of the Cross, the demand for self-denial, and the reconciliation of the sinner.[117] This means that the energy, and the direction, for the reformulation of theology and for the advancement of Christian living spring ultimately from God, not from the exclusively critical reflections of biblical or philosophical scholars. Our knowledge of God and of self must be originated and deepened solely by God the Father in Jesus the Son through the Holy Spirit. But we can only attend to one thing in one way at a time. So, at any given moment, we can regard the Word of God either signitively or critically. If we seek persuasive knowledge, all that we can do and need to do is go to the Word of God and to rely on the guidance of the Holy Spirit. With the proper humility and the loving obedience, we will experience Christ according to the measure of our faith. Our persuasive knowing will yield a cordial knowledge which will orient and coordinate our intellective knowledge. Indeed, unformulated cordial knowledge can only intimate its presence by plunging us from one intellective knowledge of things into another. Cordial knowledge received and held in this manner can be rightfully called supracritical, for it enlivens us in Christ and it secures our intellective knowledge as active knowledge unlike critical knowledge which is merely factual. This is why Calvin can say of the inward persuasion of Scripture that it is "not right to subject it to proof and reasoning" and that "we seek no proofs, no marks of genuineness upon which our judgment may lean: but we subject our judgment and wit to it as to a thing far beyond guesswork".[11] Incidentally, working scientists should find Calvin's remarks easy to accept because they relate in this very way to their own intuitive insights. They make no attempt to prove their insights. Instead, scientists assume that they are valid and then they proceed to base their researches on them. The nub of the matter is that theological knowledge is intrinsically practical knowledge involving reconciling experience. When experienced in this way, biblical studies are objectively and personally grounded on the reality and the rationality of God, being exclusively focused on Jesus Christ, the Word of God.

One fascinating feature of modern science is that it is itself a parable for the biblical student. As the actions of Mach illustrate, the scientist can only attend to one thing in one way at a time. Einstein's work shows that, if the scientist seeks sympathetic knowledge of the natural order, all that he can do and needs to do is go to the natural phenomena and rely on intuition. In their different ways, the reactions of Mach and Einstein underscore the importance of both a humble openness to new intimations of natural order and a committed obedience to sustained physical and intellectual endeavour. Equipped with this combination, the scientist can experience reality according to the measure of his faith as his intuitive insight leads him to an appropriate theoretical knowledge. Indeed, unformulated intuitive knowledge can only intimate its presence by plunging the scientist from one theoretical knowledge of things into another. Intuitive knowledge received and held in this manner can be properly called supracritical, for it activates the scientist in his researches and it secures his theoretical knowledge as active knowledge, unlike merely factual, critical knowledge. The scientist never subjects his intuitive knowledge to proof and reasoning. He seeks no proofs, no marks of genuineness upon which his judgment of intuitive insight may lean, but rather he submits his judgment and his skills to that insight as to a thing far beyond guesswork. He subjects to proof and reasoning the resulting explicit expressions, the theoretical formulations, flowing from it. The heart of the matter is that scientific knowledge is practical knowledge involving sympathetic experience of reality. When experienced in this way, scientific research is objectively and personally grounded on the reality and the rationality of the universe, being exclusively focused on the natural order. In the light of this parable, it is clear that Calvin's theology is far from outmoded. In fact, there is much to be said for the claim that Calvin is a theologian for the modern scientist.

CHAPTER 6

OBJECTIVE KNOWLEDGE

B Y regarding modern science as a parable for the biblical
student, we have already taken a significant step towards
recognising that a proper, objective, personal grounding of
biblical studies on the reality, the rationality, and the
intelligibility of God will engender not antagonism but
openness to the cultural achievements of humankind.
According to Calvin, "the mind of man, though fallen and
perverted from its wholeness, is nevertheless clothed and
ornamented with God's excellent gifts. If we regard the
Spirit of God as the sole fountain of truth, we shall neither
reject the truth itself, nor despise it wherever it shall appear,
unless we wish to dishonour the Spirit of God. For by
holding the gifts of the Spirit in light esteem, we condemn
and reproach the Spirit himself." [118] Calvin's words leave us
in no doubt that the seeker of persuasive truth draws from
the unique spring of truth, the Holy Spirit, as the
independent, objective, dynamic intelligibility of God. By
relying on this spring alone, our very persons are integrated
and grounded on the truth of God. But, as Calvin reminds
us, the disruption of the person is a direct consequence of the
Fall. Sin is strictly about man's relationship to God: it
produces an existential, not just a moral, disintegration,
disfiguring the soul, mind, and body of man. As man is split
asunder like an atom of personality by his wilful denial of the
persuasive truth of God, his "exceptional gifts" completely
disappear and his "excellent gifts" are warped almost
beyond recognition in the annihilating collision of divine and
human wills. Man's supranatural gifts are taken away and
his natural gifts are corrupted. [119] Although those natural
gifts are deprived of their original use, they are still the
"excellent gifts" of God. The Holy Spirit can work through

them and so, if we recognise the Holy Spirit as the only
source of truth, we shall remain open to his work wherever
truth is disclosed. In other words, we are required in
faithfulness to the ministry of the Holy Spirit to hold the
cultural achievements of humankind in appropriately high
regard.

Calvin is firmly convinced that the human intellect
working under its own steam cannot possibly attain a sound
knowledge of God and of self essentially because it cannot
reach a persuasion of God's saving benevolence.[120] None the
less, he expresses an intense appreciation of an extensive
range of disciplines, including mathematics, medicine, law,
logic, and philosophy. "We cannot read the writings of the
ancients on these subjects", writes Calvin, "without great
admiration. We marvel at them because we are compelled to
recognise how pre-eminent they are. But shall we count
anything praiseworthy or noble without recognising at the
same time that it comes from God? Let us be ashamed of
such ingratitude, into which not even the pagans fell, for
they confessed that the gods had invented philosophy, law,
and all useful arts [which in Calvin's day included the
sciences]."[118] Without hesitation, Calvin refers what
fragmented excellence there is in human culture to God who
has bestowed it.[97] It is God who fills, moves, and enlivens all
things by the power of the Holy Spirit. He does so according
to the nature which he has bestowed upon each kind by the
law of creation. Therefore, "If the Lord has willed that we
be helped in physics, dialectic, mathematics, and other like
disciplines, . . . let us use this assistance. For if we neglect
God's gift freely offered in these arts, we ought to suffer just
punishment for our sloth."[121] And true to his word, Calvin
praises and commends the study of science repeatedly
throughout his commentaries and in *The Institutes*.

Resurgent creationism can draw little comfort from the
words of Calvin. In fact, his words are probably a constant
source of embarrassment to it. Its efforts to dominate the
teaching of modern science by literalist interpretations of the
Scriptures oppose the theology of Calvin in fundamental
respects. As we have already discussed at some length,

Calvin refuses to have anything to do with all systems of biblical interpretation that impose their own inflexible concepts on the biblical material. His studies clearly dissociate him especially from any system whose every word is given a forced literalness which commands an absolute authority independent of context or purpose. On the contrary, Calvin recognises, for example, that the Scriptures speak to us of the creation of the world and that they refer to the law of creation. The Bible does not discuss theories of the origin of the universe or of the laws of nature. Written by theologians, not by scientists, its purpose is to point us to our profound relationship to God, humankind, and the rest of creation, not to improve our scientific knowledge. In his commentary on Genesis, Calvin makes this amply clear: "For as it became a theologian, he [Moses] had respect to *us* rather than to the *stars*."[122] In reference to the gifts of the specialist, Calvin advises us that "ingenious men are to be honoured who have expended useful labour on this subject [astronomy]". He also reminds us that the needs of the ordinary person are not neglected for "the Spirit of God opens a common school for all". Any differences resulting from the two avenues of learning have to be considered in the light of the knowledge that "Moses wrote in a popular style things which, without instruction, all ordinary persons, endued with common sense, are able to understand; but astronomers investigate with great labour whatever the sagacity of the human mind can comprehend. Nevertheless, this study is not to be reprobated, nor this science to be condemned, because some frantic persons are wont boldly to reject whatever is unknown to them. For astronomy is not only pleasant, but also very useful to be known: it cannot be denied that this art unfolds the admirable wisdom of God."[123]

Consequently, we learn from Calvin that we would be in multiple error if we asserted on the basis of a literalist interpretation of the Scriptures such things as 'the earth is only a few thousand years old' or 'each and every species is associated with a specific act of creation'. First, the Bible should not be exposed to ridicule by taking literally all its statements. It is not a collection of inerrant religious statements or facts to be read and manipulated in some mechanistic manner. Without the guidance of the Holy Spirit the student of Scripture encounters the sterility of merely human constructions. Secondly, the Bible should not be misconstrued as a scientific textbook. The scriptural corpus does not detail for us the mechanisms of the scientific origins of the universe or of life. It provides us with a personal knowledge of God's plan of salvation for humankind. Its unique purpose is to serve as the instrument of the Holy Spirit who schools us in our personal knowledge of God and of self. Thirdly, the ministry of the Spirit of God through the instrumentality of modern science should not be denied merely on the basis of fundamentalist modes of human thought. According to Calvin, if the excellent gifts of humankind are employed by the sciences, then they can unfold the admirable wisdom of God. Since he leaves us in little doubt about the priority of the Scriptures and about the usefulness of science, we have no excuse for separating faith and reason in a misguided creationist attempt to subject to proof what lies beyond proof and reasoning, namely, the ministry of the Holy Spirit.

The root error of creationism is that it does not take seriously enough the work of the Holy Spirit. Its sterile literalism eclipses the ministry of the Spirit of God and it drives a wedge between faith and reason. Faith is blind without reason and reason is immobile without the kinetics of faith. Thus blind faith perceives nothing and pure reason goes nowhere. In the absence of persuasive knowledge, intellective knowledge does not exist and its counterfeit explicit knowledge is neither oriented nor coordinated. So the creationist has to find for himself another way of integrating this explicit knowledge. The creationist literature provides ample evidence of how difficult it is for even intellectually gifted individuals to create a successful integration of the literalist data of 'creation-science'. Strangely, the absence of a systematic creation-science with its own recognisable methods does not deter creationists in their misinterpretations of well-founded scientific theories and of well-established methods.[124] Having effectively denied the activity of the Holy Spirit in the interpretation of Scripture, it is hardly surprising to learn that creationists combine blind faith and the abuse of human reasoning in order to reject the legitimate findings of modern science. This lack of discernment is an offence against the ministry of the Holy Spirit, a dishonouring which cannot be justified even in reaction to scientists who smuggle metaphysical notions like materialism into their arguments. In creationism humankind has found yet another way of distorting our objective and personal knowledge of God and of self.

On what grounds can we claim, for instance, that our apprehension of modern biological evolution is objective? Certain aspects of the biologist's understanding have withstood the repeated tests of time and the rapid advances not only of biology but of the natural sciences in general. But we concentrate on one particular aspect since this is sufficient for our present limited purposes. The original concept of the emergence of new forms of life has deepened to such an extent that it has been extended to give biological evolution a place within the vast spectrum of cosmic evolution. By drawing on the resources of the special sciences with their impressive variety of methods, we discover cosmic evolution. There is a continuous development of matter from the 'big bang' origin of the universe fifteen to eighteen thousand million years ago, through the undifferentiated hot soup of elementary matter and radiation that allowed the formation of atoms and small molecules,[125] on to the prebiotic planetary soup containing large self-replicating molecular structures that initiated the development of the great diversity of living forms.[126] The quality and the quantity of this evidence are such that it is no longer possible to attack biological evolution in isolation from other aspects of modern science. Its place within an objective scientific apprehension of the universe is as secure as any scientific theory can be, always remembering of course the tales of Euclidean geometry and Newton's Laws of Motion. Besides fitting relatively neatly into the general scientific picture, biological evolution is firmly established as an objective instrument of biological apprehension. For instance, the interrelatedness of all living organisms has been confirmed on the basis of their biological mechanisms, of the chemically arbitrary, but universally specific, genetic code, and of the congruity of the independently determined relationships between species on morphological grounds and by the comparative analyses of their proteins. Moreover, if recent developments are anything to go by, biological evolution still has a lot of new life left in it. The exciting studies of Ilya Prigogine and his Brussels School give us an new understanding of self-organising systems in states appreciably removed from thermodynamic equilibrium.[127] Those researches have shown that, in many cases, simple behaviour patterns in advanced biological systems can be investigated using mathematical procedures that are applicable to inorganic chemical reactions. Although similarity is neither equality nor equivalence, this important work does indicate that the ordered complexity of biological systems is probably due to self-organising, non-equilibrium, physical processes. In other words, it seems that the emergence of life is an inevitable, objective feature of the physical world. In the light of all this scientific knowledge, it is simply absurd to deny the validity of biological evolution on any grounds other than sound scientific theory. Instead of trying to devise an 'alternative science', many Christians could be more gainfully employed by following Calvin's solid advice. We can take pleasure and instruction from the profound thought that we are self-consciously, self-organising organisms. This means, among other things, that we are self-consciously a product of cosmic evolution and that some of us can personally research in biology in order to apprehend the objective laws of nature, from which knowledge we can all benefit.

What we and the creationists would do well to bear constantly in mind is that Calvin always speaks as a redeemed person who is firmly persuaded of God's benevolence in Jesus Christ. He believes solidly that, while sin leaves no spot unblemished in the life of fallen humanity, redeemed humanity guided by the Holy Spirit is free to pick any of the fruits of fallen man's culture and to choose to use them in the loving service of God and of man. The Spirit of God discloses to him the persuasive truth through the Word of God. By this very means the redeemed person can be led like Calvin to a grateful, practical recognition of the excellent gifts of humankind. Indeed, we have already acknowledged that Calvin is deeply indebted to Renaissance humanism for much of his knowledge of philosophy, logic, law, history *etc.,* and also for some of his methods as a theologian and a scriptural exegete. For him, his indebtedness is not a source of embarrassment but one of appreciative wonder. Calvin is persuaded that man, his natural gifts, and his immediate world point beyond themselves through the Holy Spirit to the Word of God. And, as if to endorse permanently his solid persuasion, history obliges us with two highly gifted men who, separated by only a few years but working independently, displaced man from the centre of reality. In 1536 Calvin produced his Christocentric theology and in 1543 Copernicus published his heliocentric astronomical theory, two events based on something far greater than merely critical knowledge. Prefiguring the results of Gödel, both systems appealed openly and deliberately to an objective rationality that transcended the explicit sphere of humankind. The origins of modern science and of reformed theology share a common basis in faith, an uncompromising commitment to unspecifiable, objective knowledge.

Hopefully by this stage in our discussion, the contrast between a critical understanding of God and of self and a persuasive apprehension is quite sharp. Only formulated knowledge can be derived from specifiable premises according to definite rules of logic. Systematised, explicit knowledge can always be critically studied with a view to increasing its internal consistency and its interior economy. Indeed, the most important function of critical thought is to test explicit, logical processes by following their chains of reasoning in search of weak links.[128] But purely critical knowledge can tell us nothing about the external consistency, or the external economy, of systematised, explicit knowledge. By the external consistency of a system of knowledge we mean the extent to which the system is consistent with the general body of fundamental findings and of principal theories of the particular discipline. For example, we can say that the external consistency of biological evolution is exceptionally high because it is consistent with cosmic evolution, or that the external consistency of Calvin's theology is remarkably great because it is consistent with the Scriptures. By the external economy of a system of knowledge we mean the power of the system to explain its domain of validity. For example, the external economy of biological evolution is considerable because it explains a whole range of biological findings, although it is not notable for its specific predictions of them. Similarly, the external economy of Calvin's theology is prodigious because it embraces the sum of religion in all its parts. Since purely critical knowledge cannot cope with those aspects of systematised, explicit knowledge, we can say that the critical knowledge of the scientist, or the Christian, appears as a relatively small lighted area of the knowledge of reality surrounded by immense darkness. This tiny spot of explicit knowledge can be scrutinised under the control of critical reflection. In this respect, the theologian resembles the working scientist who is so often acutely aware of the severe limitations of his theoretical and empirical knowledge, an explicit knowledge that can always be critically reappraised.

In contrast to critical knowledge, cordial knowledge illumines for us the divine image of the invisible God through the supracritical acceptance of its unreasoned disclosures. Similarly, Einstein and Polanyi explain scientific apprehension in terms of an intuitive knowledge that casts light on the rationality of the universe through the supracritical acceptance of its unreasoned insights. This integral awareness or unformulated, unspecifiable knowledge of God and of self enables intellective knowledge to function as the articulate complement of cordial knowledge. But this special type of explicit knowledge is oriented and coordinated within us by the Holy Spirit in order to point us beyond itself to the true image of the transcendent God. Being shaped from beyond us, intellective knowledge is objective but, being fashioned within us, it is also personal. We can say that intellective knowledge is the workmate of cordial knowledge which always occupies the driving seat. But if this is the case, if the cordial component of persuasive knowledge predominates, how are we supposed to react to the pre-eminently critical approach to biblical studies of so many theologians and of sizeable numbers of the clergy? Surely, we also must identify with the seemingly pervasive preference which has urged the modern Christian mind to overcome its uncritical acceptance of tradition and doctrine. It seems outrageous even to hint that we should turn our backs on the resulting, vast, public record of articulate Christian knowledge, especially in favour of something as nebulous as persuasive knowlege. Moreover, in the wake of our rapidly advancing supertechnology with its ever-increasing applications to literary and biblical studies, it appears to be well nigh inevitable that we accept as our urgent goal the establishment and the presentation of a precise, logical system of theological knowledge, if our theology is to have any realistic hope of being relevant in this newly emerging age. What appears to be required is a critical account of the biblical contents which has been thoroughly decontaminated from any personal participation, the latter being considered as a noxious impurity to be scrupulously eliminated.[129]

Yet this exalted valuation of strictly formalised theological knowledge can be shown to be self-contradictory. It is certainly true that the scholar who is provided with the critical apparatus of modern biblical studies enjoys a striking logical, if not intellectual, superiority over the ordinary Christian. The latter is equipped for the most part only with native ability coupled to humility and obedience as he searches the Scriptures.[130] But, as Calvin points out, it is always better to limp along the latter path than to dash with all speed outside of it.[44] Sometimes the committed explorer's fumbling progress turns out to be a much finer spiritual achievement than the well-versed traveller's dispassionate survey.[128] Even the most erudite student of Scripture, or the most exalted church leader, cannot advance in Christ unless he is first persuaded that the Son of God came, not to give us a formal, representational knowledge of a superior world, but to save us from a sinful terminus in this world. Calvin tells us that we must search the Scriptures "in order that we might know to what end Christ was sent by the Father and what he has brought to us".[131] This must be the goal of all our biblical studies without exception. Otherwise, we are without the centre of reference that gives our relative knowledge objectivity and we are cast adrift clinging desperately to some form of relativism on the high seas of subjectivity.

The plain fact is that "as long as Christ is far from us and we dwell apart from him, all that he has suffered and accomplished for the human race is useless and unavailing to us".[132] This is true for all that we do, including our study of Scripture and our systematisation of theology. Unless the persuasive truth of God imparts existential and relational knowledge, even the genius wanders among his futile fantasies. His study of Scripture is at most an extensive literary project and his systematic theology is an imaginative elaboration of an exercise in logic. However, if his biblical and theological studies centre in the supreme reality that "in the Person of Jesus Christ perfect salvation is found",[133] then these studies engage the complete person of the scholar. That is, our affections are kept within the bounds of reason, our senses are tempered in the right order, and we are empowered to refer our excellence to the exceptional gifts bestowed on us by the Father through Jesus Christ our Lord.[97] The profound truth is not that God gives us an increased intellect or an improved human nature or even a part of himself, but that he gives us none other than the Second Adam. God comes to us in our own humanity. The intellect and the human nature that we have already become instrumental in God's gracious hand as we are persuaded that Jesus is the Second Adam. But without Christ the most gifted biblical student, or the most brilliant theological scholar, remains only an interested spectator, standing on

the sidelines of the objective ground of reality and watching
the personal participation in the persuasive truth.

We have seen how the biblical mechanic is so readily
trapped by his own literalist system simply because he
regards the Word of God as a source of truths to be read
mechanically and applied inflexibly. He cannot see past the
literalist instrument of Scripture which he idolises. Now we
look at the other extreme. We see how the biblical liberalist
sinks himself in the morass of the relativism of all
knowledge. Like the biblical mechanic, the biblical liberalist
or the biblical relativist also sees the Scriptures as an
instrument. But he is so preoccupied with his own pedantic
applications of extrinsic material, which are supposedly
relevant to the meaning of Scripture, and which biblical
relativism continues, and will continue, to multiply, that he
has little or no time for the Word of God as the divine, and
therefore unique, instrument of the Holy Spirit.[134] In order
to outline the grave dangers of biblical relativism for modern
biblical studies, we attempt to highlight the salient features
of the biblical relativist's approach against the background
of some recent, thought-provoking advances in modern
science. First, we consider briefly some elementary aspects
of Special Relativity, then we scratch the surface of some of
the more obvious cosmological consequences of General
Relativity.

Many problems have arisen concerning the meaning of
the special theory of relativity simply because the name
Special Relativity does not adequately reflect the essential
nature of this theory. Indeed, it is common knowledge
among scientists that Hermann Minkowski was quick to
object to this name and also that Einstein later admitted that
he would have preferred to call it the theory of invariance.
Those scientists had sound scientific reasons for their
objections but there were also solid, non-scientific ones. In
particular, the name Special Relativity suggests that the
content of the theory is fundamentally about 'relativity'. But
relativity is also associated with relativism which is the
theory of the relativity of knowledge. In the latter context,
relativity means subjectivism. Consequently, many people

tended to interpret wrongly the contents of Special Relativity as providing evidence of a powerful physical theory which supported the doctrine of the relativity of all knowledge, a doctrine that also lies at the heart of modern biblical liberalism. The strange knowledge of Einstein's new world of spacetime required an effort that not everyone was prepared to make. But certain features of the theory had an immediate appeal, especially when they were taken out of context. For instance, many scholars who believed in relativism were impressed by the fact that, according to Special Relativity, people could disagree with impunity about when and where events happened.

This unfortunate name gained general acceptance largely because it originated from the name of a fundamental scientific postulate or principle put forward independently by Albert Einstein and by Henri Poincaré at the turn of the century. This fundamental postulate, known as "The Principle of Relativity", represented a rejection of the notion of an absolute, motionless frame of reference associated with the then-postulated electromagnetic ether, a notion which had been introduced by scientists in order to explain certain optical and electrodynamic phenomena. This principle formed the basis of a new theoretical approach to space and time. In his now-famous paper, *"On the Electrodynamics of Moving Bodies"*,[111] Einstein states that "the unsuccessful attempts to discover any motion of the earth relatively to a 'light medium' suggests that the phenomena of electrodynamics as well as of mechanics possess no properties corresponding to the idea of absolute rest. They suggest rather that, as has already been shown . . . the same laws of electrodynamics and optics will be valid for all frames of reference for which the equations of mechanics hold good. We will raise this conjecture (the purport of which will hereafter be called the 'Principle of Relativity') to the status of a postulate."[135] Almost simultaneously, Poincaré formulated his analogous 'Relativity Postulate': "This impossibility of experimentally demonstrating the absolute motion of the Earth appears to be a general law of Nature; it is reasonable to assume the existence of this law, which we shall call the *relativity postulate,* and to assume that it is universally valid."[136] Thus from its inception, the name 'Principle of Relativity' was associated with the rejection of the concepts of an absolute frame of reference and of an absolute motion relative to a system at absolute rest. It is, therefore, very tempting to interpret Special Relativity as a powerful theory which is firmly based on physical evidence and solidly opposed to the concepts of an absolute frame of knowledge and of an objective knowing relative to an absolute knower. Needless to say, many people have found their own reasons and methods of yielding to this particular temptation. But no matter what the reasons are, sin is sin even against a scientific theory.

Special Relativity sprang from the ground of experimental science. Yet it opens up a world which preserves only a kind of union of space and time as an independent reality. In this world, the forms of the laws of nature remain unaltered if the system of reference in space and time is changed. We say that the laws of nature are invariant. But for any observer the system of reference in space and in time is not unequivocally determined by the phenomena. And any two observers will see different projections in space and in time of the same phenomena, although both observers will agree that those phenomena obey the same formal laws of nature. Similarly, we may say that Calvin's theology sprang from the ground of his personal experience of the Word of God. His theology indicates for us a life in the Word incarnate, which involves only a kind of union of the human word and the divine Word as an independent reality, a union more commonly recognised as the ministry of the Holy Spirit. In this realm of life in Christ, the doctrine of Scripture remains unaltered, if the theological system of reference in word and Word is changed. We may say that the doctrine of Scripture is invariant. But for any biblical student his theological system is not fully determined by the biblical events. And any two biblical students will experience different, personal apprehensions in word and in Word of the same biblical events, although both will recognise that those events conform to the same divine doctrine of Scripture. The possibility of such a parallel between the thought of Einstein and that of Calvin greatly intensifies our interest in Special Relativity.

Hermann Minkowski was the first to place on record his complaint that the term 'relativity postulate' was too feeble to do justice to the preeminent requirement of invariance that the new theory' of spacetime demanded. Having set the record straight, he then stated: "Since the postulate comes to mean that only the four-dimensional world in space and time is given by phenomena, but that the project in space and in time may still be undertaken with a certain degree of freedom, I should prefer to call it the *postulate of the absolute world* (or briefly, the world-postulate)."[137] Thus Minkowski's work left the scientific world in no doubt about the inadequacy of the names Special Relativity and Principle of Relativity. He spelled out that those names do not reflect the essential content of a theory that is fundamentally a theory of invariance. Without going into unnecessary details, we may safely say that modern scientists who use Special Relativity see the door to its real content turning on the hinge that the laws of nature are invariant. The forms of those laws remain totally independent of the reference frame of any observer. There is no such thing as a preferred frame of reference. And, since the laws of nature do not depend on the point of view of the observer, there are no valid grounds for assuming that Special Relativity lends support to the notion of the complete relativity of all physical knowledge. In fact, according to Special Relativity, the laws of nature are powerful, invariant, scientific expressions of the rationality of the universe; that is, they symbolise objective knowledge of an independently ordered reality.

Extending our parallel, we may say that only the Christofocal theology in word and Word is given by the biblical events, but that the human separation in word and in Word is undertaken with God-given free will. The essential content of this theology is, however, the invariance of the doctrine of Scripture. The door to Calvin's theology turns on the hinge that the doctrine of Scripture remains invariant which means that it is totally independent of the theological reference system of the biblical student. There is no such thing as an infallible or absolute, theological reference system. And, since the doctrine of Scripture does not depend on the theological perspective of the biblical student, there are no valid grounds for assuming that Calvin's theology lends support to the notion of the complete relativity of all religious knowledge. In fact, according to Calvin, the divine doctrine of Scripture is the invariant expression of the law of God who is Jesus Christ; it is the objective knowledge of God the Creator and the Redeemer who is Reality. This astounding correspondence between the basic concepts of Special Relativity and Calvin's theology not only helps us to understand the irrelevance of biblical relativism, but it also reveals Calvin as a distinguished theologian with thoroughly modern modes of thought.

We are privileged to live in the age of post-Einsteinian cosmology. As early as the third and second centuries before Christ, Epicurus, Aristarchus, and Hipparchus tickled the notion of an infinite universe whose centre was not the earth. Then cosmology was in embryo, so to speak. But it was not until the illustrious Copernicus had theoretically displaced the earth from the centre of the universe that the modern science of cosmology was born. His work coupled to the invention of the telescope encouraged a quantitative exploration of our solar system and the stars. The second great phase of modern cosmology was inaugurated by Einstein as he presented his model of an isotropic and homogeneous universe. By homogeneous we mean that the universe looks the same to any observer wherever he is located; by isotropic, that the universe looks the same in all directions to any observer. With his cosmological work as the rational scientific application of General Relativity, Einstein brought the universe as a tangible object, as a concrete reality, within scientific reach. Thus along with the development of General Relativity from Special Relativity, there came the exciting realisation that the very structure of the universe could be scientifically investigated. Einstein conceived General Relativity as a theory to cope with the large, perhaps infinite, scale of the universe as a whole. It was possible to study quantitatively the structure of the universe, provided of course its overall structure was sufficiently simple. Einstein assumed the uniformity of the universe on the large scale despite the fact that it appears to be exceedingly complex in our immediate neighbourhood. However, when its structure is viewed on a grand [cosmological] scale, it takes on an entirely different complexion. As it turns out, by first observing the cosmic beam in the cosmologist's eye, we can see how to remove the terrestrial speck from our own.

Einstein led the modern way to a consistent cosmology based on gravitational interaction. But there are still many important, unanswered questions, like whether the universe is open or closed. Nevertheless, this work reveals, at the very least, that the notion of the universe as a whole is a workable scientific concept which promises to have a long and exciting life. This concept is amenable to both experimental investigation and theoretical inquiry. Despite the fact that the scientist has yet to produce the elusive Unified Field Theory which will be valid for all known [and as yet unknown] interactions, including the electromagnetic, the weak, the nuclear, and the gravitational types, he can presently concentrate on some very intriguing quantitative features of current models of the universe. For instance, is the total mass of the universe finite or infinite? The mean density of matter in cosmic spaces seems to hold the measurable answer to this question. But there is always at least one fly in the ointment. There is the knowledge that General Relativity, though successfully tested within our solar system, must break down when densities become so high that quantum gravitational effects become important. The significant point remains, however, that the cosmologist can test the prediction of any cosmological model against an experimentally determined value of the mean density of matter. Not only is there an independently ordered reality of universal dimensions, this reality yields quantitatively objective knowledge when it is scientifically investigated. The findings of modern cosmology expose the fallacy that the theory of relativity supports the doctrine of the relativity of all knowledge. The comparative successes of modern cosmological models remind us that to be simple is wise but to be wise is not simple. Perhaps the salutary scientific lesson for the biblical relativist is that, if we depend exclusively on our own powers of human reasoning, then we will be lost in the resulting morass of relativism, whereas if we remain alert to the disclosures of independently ordered reality, then we will be found amidst the continuing, enlivening pursuit of objective knowledge.

One of the most spectacular manifestations of the quantitativeness of the structure of the universe is the scientific evidence for its origin. The uniformity of the universe on the large scale was not the only thing that Einstein assumed. He also assumed a static, non-evolving universe which proved to be wrong. Not long after Einstein had published his cosmological treatment as a logical scientific application of General Relativity,[138] W. de Sitter produced a related model. The Einstein universe appeared to be unstable with its slightest disturbance sending it into an expanding phase and carrying it ultimately into the de Sitter form. In the de Sitter universe there was no uniform distribution of matter and this model predicted that matter would accelerate away from the origin. Thus the de Sitter universe was subject to expanding and required the recession velocity of matter to be proportional to its distance from the earth. This suggested that astronomers should look for the systematic recession of distant matter.[139] In fact, the spiral galaxies tended to have velocities away from the earth, as shown by their red shifts.[139] But this feature had remained a mere curiosity because it seemed to support an untenable view of the earth as the centre of the universe. The curiosity turned rapidly into scientific inquiry, however, as it was realised that perhaps the nature of the universe as a whole varied with time. The thought of the universe being time-conditioned and having a specific age met with a mixed reception in the scientific community as many metaphysical skeletons popped out of the cupboards. The metaphysical frightening spectre for many people was the possibility that the universe was not only quantitatively objective but comprehensively contingent.

In fact, there are several sources of evidence which suggest strongly that the universe has a finite age. When taken together, they underscore the quantitativeness of the universe as a whole while pointing to the universality of modern scientific methods and affirming the existence of an independently ordered reality. If the cosmological red-shift is due to the expansion of the universe, then the age of the universe will be of the order of twenty thousand million years. Radioactive dating of isotopes of the oldest rocks on the earth, from the moon, and in meteorites, gives ages in good agreement at around five thousand million years, a figure also estimated from calculations of the structure and the evolution of the sun. Using the same techniques, the material in our galaxy as a whole yields an age of about twenty thousand millions years, and the ages of other nearby galaxies are of the same order, independent of galaxy type. Even the romantic versions of 'Custer's Last Stand' and 'The Charge of The Light Brigade' pale into insignificance when placed alongside the current saga of the resistance of creationists to this kind of scientific evidence for the great age of the universe.

Undoubtedly one of the most decisive factors in the advance of recent cosmology, however, was the discovery of the 2.7 degrees Kelvin cosmic background radiation by A. A. Penzias and R. W. Wilson in 1965. If we point a telescope at a region of the sky free of bright sources, we can measure the total integrated background intensity of radiation from all sources in the sky at all distances. As these scientists discovered, the most striking result is the 2.7 degrees Kelvin black-body background radiation. Although other more complex explanations can be given, the simplest one is that this background radiation is a relic of the fireball phase of an isotropic, big bang universe. During such a phase, radiation would be the dominant form of energy in the universe. The observed isotropy of this radiation must date from long times in the past, and it places severe limits on any anisotropic model of the universe. Further evidence for a fireball phase could be the fact that the stars in our galaxy appear to have formed from an initial mixture containing 27 per cent helium, 73 per cent hydrogen, by mass. Since nearly all the remaining elements could be formed within the interior of stars, the universe could have started as pure hydrogen with helium forming in some prestellar fireball phase. The most stunning thing, perhaps, is that the cosmologist can calculate the abundances of the chemical elements formed in the early universe from comparatively few assumed initial conditions, for example, one proton and one neutron for every thousand million photons at a temperature of one hundred thousand million degrees Kelvin.[140] He can also extrapolate to the lepton, hadron, and quantum eras, states which existed only tiny fractions of a second after the hot big bang. The evidence is overwhelming. The universe is, in fact, an expanding system with a definite evolution scenario.

We see that the scientist can already provide the first approximation to the large scale structure of the universe including the dynamics of expansion. He is presently attempting the elucidation of the physical content of the evolving phases. We may say that the cosmologist is within range of scientifically determining the age, the isotropy, the homogeneity, the shape, the size, the mean density of matter, the chemical constitution, and the evolution of the universe. Certainly, the quantitativeness of the universe has been firmly established using a vast array of scientific methods. Indeed, it is small wonder that modern cosmology with its popular presentations has fired the imagination of humankind, for it is truly an exciting venture into unknown, but knowable, independently ordered reality. The modern cosmologist offers us a realist knowledge of the invariant laws of nature and their domains of validity. This knowledge includes theory-laden data and empirically loaded theory. It is none the less objective knowledge of the contingent universe and as such it opposes directly the doctrine of the relativity of all knowledge. Indeed, the models of the universe owe their very existence to the fundamental recognition, not just that there is an independently ordered reality, but that the rationality of this reality is apprehensible to us. As Einstein himself wrote: "Certain it is that a conviction, akin to religious feeling, of the rationality or intelligibility of the world lies behind all scientific work of a higher order."[105]

The intelligibility of the universe stretches from beyond the veil of microphysics which presently obscures our view of the beginning of the hot, big bang universe out to the horizon of the universe beyond which events cannot yet have any effect on us because of the finite speed of light. This tells us nothing less than that, conceivably within our galaxy, humankind can uniquely cooperate with nature. It reminds us that we may choose to annihilate intelligent life on our own planet but it makes equally plain the fact that we cannot hope to dominate the universe. The real choice is between the free exploration of its rationality or the limiting exploitation of its quantitativeness. The former acknowledges and exercises what Einstein called "the mysterious harmony of nature into which we are born".[106] This harmony allows "the human mind to construct forms independently before we can find them in things".[15] Einstein reminds us that "knowledge cannot spring from experience alone but only from the comparison of the inventions of the intellect with observed fact".[15] Clearly, the manipulative exploitation of the quantitativeness of the universe was never a viable option for him, nor should it be for us, since such exploitation presupposes wrongly that we can stamp without retribution our prejudices on the processes of nature. In fact, by visiting the exigencies of our unguided minds on the universe, we check our own progress in the knowledge of the interdependence of things and we ignore the work of Gödel which warns us that all of our conceptual inventions or systems are either creatively or destructively incomplete. Indeed, the further we penetrate the rationality of the universe, the more obvious it becomes that respect, not abuse, is the way to treat this wonderful world. Incidentally, if we get the scientific attitude right, then there can be hope that some day a genuinely ecological one will emerge. But if modern science is led into the exploitative labyrinth of relativism, then ecology is likely to remain a political tool until the sun dies.

Just as the sagacious acknowledgement of the invariance of the laws of nature unlocked for Einstein, and therefore for modern cosmology, the wonders of the universe as a whole, so the profound recognition of the ageless validity of the law of God opens for Calvin, and therefore for reformed theology, the miraculous freedom of the whole of Christian living. We may say that, for Calvin, the continuing need of the law as a guide and a norm remains invariant throughout the life of the Christian. In the Ten Commandments Calvin discovered principles that are universally valid. His exact words are that the Decalogue is "a perfect pattern of righteousness" and "one everlasting rule to live by".[141] They are the laws of redeemed human nature, which God has graciously gifted to the universal Church. Given in the Scriptures and interpreted through the Holy Spirit, the law of God is indispensable for Christian living. "For, considered in itself, it [the law] is the way of eternal life; and, except for our depravity, is capable of bringing salvation to us. . . . Christ declared that he taught no other plan of life than what had been taught of old in the law of the Lord. So also he attested God's law to be the doctrine of perfect righteousness, and at the same time confuted false reports so he might not seem by some new rule of life to incite the people to desert the law."[142]

Here Calvin states that Christ "attested God's law to be the doctrine of perfect righteousness", so we may confidently assume that, whatever he recognises as the law of God, it is the doctrine which, if perfectly fulfilled, will lead to the person's right relationship with God. Indeed, Calvin understands that Christ himself regarded the law of redeemed human nature as invariant, and that, with a love unsurpassable in intent and extent, Christ fulfilled the law as God's expressed will to humankind. Thus, as we noted earlier the divine doctrine of Scripture is the invariant expression of the law of God who is Jesus Christ. The law of God is the objective knowledge of God the Creator and God the Redeemer. Because "God has revealed his will in the law",[143] Calvin can state that the followers of Christ "are taught to live not according to their own whim but according to God's will".[33] This understanding of the law amplifies his references to such things as the unique, comprehensive government of the Christian life by the will of God. For example, "He alone has truly denied himself who has so totally resigned himself to the Lord that he permits every part of his life to be governed by God's will."[34]

At one extreme, the biblical mechanic "who would confine his understanding of the law within the narrowness of the words deserves to be laughed at".[87] At the other, there stands the biblical relativist defying anyone who "bids reason give way to, submit and subject itself to the Holy Spirit so that man himself may no longer live but hear Christ living and reigning within him [Galatians 2: 20]."[144] The best interpreter of the law is Christ[145] who came from beyond the veil of creation which shields our sinful natures from the holiness of God's thoughts and ways. Christ has poured out his Spirit upon humankind from beyond the horizon of death which no longer has the last word in our lives because of the triumph of the light of the world. This tells us nothing less than that humankind can uniquely commune with God, even if there are more than one form of intelligent life per galaxy in the universe. It reminds us that we may choose to annihilate the intelligent life we have but it makes equally plain the fact that there is no spiritual future in do-it-yourself theology. The real choice is between the free fellowship of the Holy Spirit or the restricting relativism of the human imagination. The former recognises the mysterious community of the universal Church into which we are reborn. This fellowship reminds us that our knowledge of God and of self cannot spring from experience alone but only from the guidance of the Holy Spirit as we base our lives on the events of salvation.

Clearly, the relativist handling of the biblical records was never a viable option for Calvin, nor should it be for us, since such covert exploitation presupposes wrongly that we can stamp without retribution our prejudices on the processes of redemption. In fact, by visiting the exigencies of

our unguided minds on the biblical corpus, we check our
own progress in the knowledge of the interdependence of all
things and we ignore the work of Gödel which warns us that
all our conceptual inventions or liberalist systems are
necessarily incomplete. Liberalist theological literature
provides us with countless examples of the many ways in
which the spiritual interdependence of the biblical events is
sacrified on the high altar of relativism. Today, it comes as
no bolt from the blue to ordinary Christians when the
Incarnation, the Virgin Birth, the Resurrection, or the
Ascension receives a direct hit from some prominent power
of human reasoning that has no biblical basis. Unquestion-
ably, there is nothing to prevent anyone reasoning on
whatever basis he chooses. But if that choice is non-biblical,
then we should have the courage of our convictions and we
should follow his arguments to their inevitable conclusion. If
we apprehend properly Calvin's theology and what he
means by the doctrine of Scripture, then the spiritual interdependence of the biblical events implies for us that to
dismiss, for example, the Resurrection is actually tampering
with the Gospel as a whole because it cannot match his own
supposedly superior, human reasoning. Of course, there is
always the alternative scientific response which openly
acknowledges the incompleteness of human knowledge and
which humbly returns to the Scriptures in pursuit of a
persuasive apprehension of the events of salvation. Indeed,
the further we are guided into the unique motion of the word
and the Word, the more obvious it becomes that the meek
shall inherit the earth.[146]

CHAPTER 7

THE SECOND ADAM

IF Jesus Christ is the ultimate rationality, how do we make contact with the reality of God in him? How can we discover the truth of God? According to Calvin, our unaided insights and our unassisted efforts do not carry us to a recognition or an acceptance of this rationality. Christ must first reach out to us before we can respond to him in faith. Moreover, faith itself is kindled by the flame of the Holy Spirit. If faith or persuasive apprehension were merely a form of human endeavour, albeit focused on the Person and the life of Jesus Christ, then the gulf between Christ and us would not be bridged. Calvin repeated earnestly that knowledge of the heart, that is, cordial knowledge, is inspired by the Holy Spirit. He stresses that "it is true that we receive such communion through faith; since, however, it is clear that not all without distinction attain to that communion with Christ which is offered us in the Gospel, we are inevitably led to go further and to inquire into the mysterious working of the Holy Spirit through which it happens that we came to enjoy the presence of Christ and all his benefits".[132] The matter is profoundly simple. God gives us the one gift, Jesus Christ, from whom all other spiritual gifts flow. Outside of persuasive apprehension, our explicit knowledge is not truly Christofocal and, therefore, it cannot be intellective knowledge. Consequently, no matter how hard we try or how clever we are, we cannot possibly explore the riches of the Scriptures to our spiritual advancement and our personal nourishment unless we are open to the Holy Spirit who is the intelligibilty of God, so to speak.

Of course, cordial knowing cannot exist in isolation for it has no meaning or value in itself. It has saving value only by reference to its object, Jesus Christ, and it has explicit meaning only by its orientation of intellective knowledge. Like a pliant container, the cordial-intellective framework of knowledge takes on the shape of its saving content, the same Jesus Christ who fulfilled the law of God. Yet this spiritual apprehension does not form an immediate connection between Christ and us. It is flamed and fuelled by the Holy Spirit who alone secures and sustains our communion with Christ.[134] We are not mystically absorbed into some divine being. On the contrary, we are called to live real personal lives in obedience to the Gospel which teaches us to seek all things in Christ. As we obediently study the Scriptures, we come to depend utterly on the sovereign disposition of God and the paramount authority of God by recognising that our persuasive knowledge is sufficient for our present purpose in Christ. At any particular moment in our Christian life, too much knowledge would unnerve us with anticipation, while too little would paralyse us with fear. Only the Holy Spirit can provide us with economic knowledge in Christ. This knowledge promotes the spiritual growth and activity appropriate to our personal stature in Christ. Using our parallelism with Special Relativity, we can say that our personal apprehension of the Gospel events in word and in Word depends on our Christian frame of reference; that is, it depends on our theological system which is not fully determined by the Gospel events. Our personal apprehension of those events is none the less objective because we are firmly persuaded that they conform to the invariant doctrine of Scripture.

Suppose, however, that we did concede that an exact knowledge of God and of self is our supreme mental possession. It would still follow that the Christian's most distinguished act of thought consists in obediently receiving such knowledge. Even our skating on the surface of modern cosmology allows us to appreciate that the human mind is at its greatest when it is traversing uncharted domains. Working scientists must venture in faith, an activity which engages the body, mind, and spirit of the person. Such experiences reform or renew the existing articulate framework which is necessarily incomplete. They cannot be performed within this framework and so they have to rely on knowledge that cannot be proved within it. Thus we associate a kind of plunging reorientation of knowledge with transformations of frames of reference. Similarly, the biblical student must venture in faith with his whole person, if he is to experience the renewal by the Holy Spirit, and if he is to undergo the type of transformation that accompanies persuasive apprehension of the Word of God.

In order to understand a little more of what such a transformation implies for us, we must recognise that it derives from two benefits which flow from communion with Christ. Calvin explains this for us: "Two things come to us through communion with Christ. For as truly as we participate in his death, our old man is crucified by his power and the body of sin dies, so that the corruption of our first nature ceases to operate. In proportion as we participate in his resurrection we are awakened by it to newness of life corresponding to the righteousness of God. Hence I sum up the act of penitence by the one word rebirth, the object of which is that the image of God, which was defaced and almost blotted out by the transgression of Adam, should be renewed in us."[147] We have already noted that Calvin explains the Fall in terms of Adam's rejection of the Word of God. In the light of our earlier discussion of the parallelism between Calvin's theology and Special Relativity, we now express, in slightly different language, some consequences of Adam's rejection. It caused the fissure of his persuasive apprehension, leaving him with unguided understanding and ungoverned imagination. This loose association reflected the disordered and incomplete state of his fallen nature. Nevertheless, its partial successes in the adventure of life together with our inability to discover by ourselves any viable alternative are still sufficient to command our commitment to this association. In fact, the only way in which this disruption of our persons can be transcended is by our communion with Christ. As we participate in the death of Christ, that is, as we fulfil the law of God by following Christ, we are led by the Spirit of Christ to recognise, and to repent of, the disordered nature of our living and thinking.

I

The Spirit of Christ persuades us that the association of our wilful thinking and manipulative imagining must die, if the righteous seed of the apprehension of God and of self is to flourish. As we participate in the resurrection of Christ, that is, as we fulfil the law of God through the renewal in Christ of our living and thinking, we are ministered to by the Holy Spirit who guides us to a persuasive apprehension which is appropriate to our stature in Christ. Thus the image of God is renewed in us. We are in communion with Christ as the Holy Spirit enables us to see the Word of God through the words of Scripture. We have a personal and objective knowledge of Christ, a knowledge of the ultimate rationality, through the Spirit of God, the intelligibility of God, who reveals to us our knowledge of Reality, our knowledge of God and of self.

The consequence of Christ uniting himself to us is that we must live and know as those who belong to the crucified and risen Lord. Because Jesus accepted death as the wages of sin, so the life and the knowing of the fallen man in us must be slain by the piercing sword of the Spirit.[147] But Christ triumphed over death and rose again, and so we also are awakened into newness of life which includes a transformation of our knowing. Christ claims absolute sovereignty over our lives for he alone can provide us with a personal and objective knowledge of God and of self. This means that we must obey him and renounce both the life and the knowing that estrange us from God. Christians live through the Spirit of Christ and they are led by the Spirit who evokes in them persuasive apprehension and loving obedience.

We recall here two of Calvin's statements. "If we regard the Spirit of God as the sole fountain of truth, we shall neither reject the truth itself, nor despise it wherever it shall appear, unless we wish to dishonour the Spirit of God."[118] And "If the Lord has willed that we be helped in physics, dialectic, mathematics, and other like disciples, . . . let us use this assistance."[119] Those statements are better understood when the nature of modern science is viewed in the light of the crucified and risen Lord. According to Calvin, the Holy Spirit is the sole fountain of truth but Einstein refers effectively to the *intuendum* as a source of scientific insight. Calvin is firmly persuaded that the Holy Spirit works through the fragmented excellence in human culture to disclose the truth. Despite the fundamental difference in the ways that they speak of the origin of scientific insight, we can still find in Einstein's view of scientific research unintentional and unusual support for Calvin's outlook. The strange thing is that the scientist appears to work and to know after the pattern of the crucified and risen Lord, although he has no scientific need, and perhaps no particular desire, to recognise this fact. We learn from Einstein that in order to produce a new theory, the knowing and the experimentation of the scientist must be effectively slain by a mysterious intuitive relation, what we could call the sword of *intuendum*. [Einstein would not, of course, express himself in this quasi-theological way, although it does no violence to the essence of his thought.] For example, the need for greater accuracy or more extensive testing renders previously acceptable results inadequate. By the *intuendum*, the scientist is awakened into newness of research which includes a transformation of his knowing. The rationality of the universe claims absolute authority over the scientist's work for it alone can provide him with a personal and objective knowledge of independently ordered reality. This means that he must obey it and renounce both the experiments and the theories which estrange him from that reality. Scientists thrive on the *intuendum* which evokes in them a sympathetic apprehension of, and a passionate obedience to, the natural order. On comparing this scanty sketch of the working scientist with our earlier remarks on our participation in the death and in the resurrection of Christ, it becomes clearer that the *intuendum* is either the messenger of the God or the Mind behind the universe or else it represents the personification of nature. In particular, Calvin agrees fully with Einstein that the disclosures of the natural order come ultimately from the God of the universe,[148] but the two rapidly part company as Einstein talks of intuition and as Calvin relates in terms of the ministry of the Holy Spirit. In general, Calvin can find no common ground with those scholars who personify nature by placing the initiative for discovery solely with the scientist. Regardless of their differences, the thought-provoking thing is that Einstein's understanding of scientific research actually helps us to appreciate the enduring relevance of both Calvin's theology and his response to modern science.

It is extremely important that we recognise the supreme role of Christ in Calvin's theology. Christ is not like a trigger that sets in motion autonomous processes of salvation and of understanding within us. The death of the fallen man and the resurrection of the redeemed man are only realisable in the reality of the risen Lord. In him the divine image is restored, and we are privileged to share in his uniquely decisive death and resurrection. The vital point here is that we benefit derivatively from what is original in him. In so far as our lives, our hearts, and our minds are remoulded by the spiritual gifts which Christ bestows upon us, we are transformed in Christ. As the piercing sword of the Spirit progressively slays our unmasked preconceptions, prejudgments, and preoccupations, we come to know more and more fully that our knowing is due to Christ alone. For the change which Christ effects in us does not take place in a moment.[147] Nor is that change the initial stage of a graduated development towards perfection. It is rather the recognition that we must practise penitence throughout the length and breadth, the height and depth, of our lives and in every aspect and atom of our knowing.[149] The working scientist is in a privileged position to understand, if not to agree with, the need for this particular, personal requirement. Ever anew we must decide to turn away from ourselves and our knowing to God. Always we must choose to depart from our intellective knowledge of God and of self and to seek Jesus Christ. In our constant struggle with the sin that dwells within us, we are forced to recognise more extensively and more intensely our essential incapacity.[150] We are schooled to realise that the source and the strength of our new life and of our transformed knowing lie not in ourselves but in Jesus Christ in whom God has disclosed the depths of his mercy and wisdom. We are educated in the way of cordial knowing from which our intellective knowledge derives its meaning. It is not difficult, therefore, to grasp Calvin's powerful message as he comments ''that Christ who is given to us by the pure goodness of God is apprehended and appropriated by us in faith and that from our fellowship with him two graces come to us: namely, that by his sinlessness we are reconciled with God and have in heaven a gracious Father instead of a Judge, and also that sanctified by his Spirit we aspire towards an innocent and pure life.''[151] For the Christian, knowing and being go hand in hand. Fundamental mental reform can be recognised only through the same power by which Christians grow in Christ. Theological genius, if such a term is ever appropriate, seems to consist in the power to serve the uniqueness of Jesus Christ through the experience of the Holy Spirit on reading the Word of God. In other words, it is not determined by the prowess of the human intellect. The person's uses of articulate, logical operations are not ultimately decisive. It is the cordial-intellective knowing within the person that has the enlivening power. We have already acknowledged that any redeemed human capacity to regard the things of God in a persuasive way is utterly dependent upon Christ. It has nothing to do with an exclusively critical procedure. We have also indicated how we experience the things of God: persuasive power achieves those results by redeeming, reconciling, and revealing acts in our lives so as to gain greater dominion over them. There is one word that covers all of these operations. They all consist in apprehending the experience of God's saving presence, i.e., in making sense of it; the word which covers them all is simply 'wisdom'.

This apparently harmless term merits some attention for it is in fact a sharply controversial word. Polanyi has aptly reminded us that in much of our modern scholarship ''the powerful movement of critical thought has been at work to eliminate any quest for an understanding that carries with it metaphysical implications of groping for reality behind the screen of appearances''.[152] In particular, modern theological studies have been greatly influenced by the fact that modern science has been depicted as a mere description of experience, a description which, it is said, explains the facts of nature by representing discrete events as instances of general features. Thus biblical criticism has followed this lead by developing an extensive apparatus for dealing with specific narratives, incidents, and statements primarily as examples of general features like myth, miracle story, saying of Jesus *etc.* Since such representation of the biblical facts is supposed to be guided merely by an unspecified urge to simplify our account of them, rival explanations can be offered as equally viable descriptions among which we are free to choose conventionally, conveniently, or arbitrarily. Clearly, there is considerable circumstantial evidence to support the conclusion that modern biblical studies disclaim any intention of understanding the hidden nature of divine things, the deep things of God and of self.[153] Its underlying relativist philosophy condemns any such endeavour as vague, misleading, and altogether 'unscientific'. But scientists of the calibre of Einstein[154] and Polanyi[22] do not accept that science is merely a description of experience. We are not, therefore, without informed precedent in refusing to heed a doubtful warning about metaphysical implications. While it is certainly true that the growth of wisdom does lead far beyond what a strict biblical empiricism or a liberal biblical relativism regards as the domain of legitimate knowledge, we are free to reject those philosophical constructions. In any case, if they were applied consistently to the biblical contents, they would discredit any knowledge of God whatever. Yet the defectiveness of their own foundations seem to be regarded by many scholars as a small price to pay for a 'scientific' cosmetic of exceptionally poor quality. Precisely because we are exclusively interested in the reality behind the 'scientific' screen of empiricist or relativist criticism, we cannot exclude all metaphysical implications. And our acknowledgement of wisdom as a valid form of Christian knowing helps us to prevent such empiricism or relativism from mutilating our experience of the things of God and of self by reminding us that all

Christian knowledge begins and ends in our experience of Jesus Christ.

Having indicated that persuasive apprehension leads to a growth in wisdom, we turn now to a more obviously practical aspect of Calvin's theology in order to indicate the immediate relevance of his work. We consider briefly and selectively how Christian teaching and preaching lead to a persuasive development in Christ. Predictably, we concentrate on Calvin's great emphasis on the nature and the importance of preaching the Gospel. Calvin acknowledges freely that the human word of the preacher, like the human word of the Scriptures, has no intrinsic advantage and that this word cannot particularly help us. To him, "words are nothing else but signs".[155] They are essentially signitive in so far as they are instruments of God testifying to the one Word. Yet, the instrument of the human word is highly prized by Calvin. Indeed, he specifies the unadulterated proclamation of the Gospel as one of the marks of the true Church.[156] The mirror offered by the authentic preaching of God's Word reflects the countenance of God in whose wisdom "the Word goes out of the mouth of God in such a manner that likewise it goes out of the mouth of man; for God does not speak openly from heaven but employs men as his instruments".[157] We cannot possibly miss here the underlying theme of the Incarnation which holds everything together for Calvin. In Jesus Christ, the Word and the word goes out from the mouth of God and the mouth of man in uniquely indivisible unity and power. And as surely as God spoke uniquely in Jesus of Nazareth, now God speaks through persons in Christ who are his instruments and, therefore, who are given the intellective role of preaching the Gospel.

According to Calvin, the preaching of the Gospel mysteriously parallels, or rather necessarily follows, from the unique event of the Incarnation. If God were to speak to us directly, his majesty would terrify us and repel us,[158] and so, following the very pattern of the Incarnation, God condescends in the ministry of the Church to meet humankind. Persistently Christ uses earthly means in order to approach fallen humanity. He wills to speak to us through the mouths of human beings, and "the Word of God is not distinguished from the word of the prophet".[159] There is an economy of action in God's speaking through the prophets, the Second Adam, and the preachers of the Gospel. Thus in modern terms, "God does not wish to be heard but by the voice of his ministers".[160] We can say confidently that Calvin believes that the word of the preacher is accompanied by a sure testimony to persuade, to assure, and to convince the obedient hearer. This belief is of course entirely consistent with his understanding of the inspiration of Scripture and its basis in the Incarnation reminds us of Calvin's high valuation of the doctrine of Scripture to which it points. In the act of preaching the Gospel, the intellective human word is oriented by the cordial knowledge of the preacher so that the doctrine of Scripture is persuasively communicated.

The purpose of the preacher of the Gospel, who is called and appointed by God, is to expound the Scripture in the midst of the worshipping Church. As he does it, the genuine preacher believes that God will do what he did so long ago through the human words of the prophets. "Let us remember," says Calvin, "that the Gospel is preached not only by Christ's command, but by his authority and direction; in short, that we are only in his hand, and that he alone is the author of the work."[161] Again we find Calvin indicating the cordial knowing and the intellective role of the preacher while emphasising the persuasive activity of Christ through him. By the Gospel, Calvin means of course the witness of the law, of the prophets, and of the apostles of Jesus Christ.[158] Calvin's specific reference to Christ's command reminds us that we should not venerate the Gospel at a great distance or in a dispassionate manner. The genuine preacher has persuasive knowledge of the Scriptures, that is, both cordial and intellective knowledge. Christ's command is not to pass on the Gospel from one generation to the next like a treasured, critical trophy. We are not directed to admire the Gospel piously, to treat it as a source of indulgent, subjective edification, or to regard it as a piece of ancient or modern tradition. Christ's command is rather to preach the Gospel, to proclaim orally the good news of God, remembering always that authentic preaching is authoritatively directed by Christ himself. The persuasive truth of God is clothed in intellective human words for "among the many noble endowments with which God has adorned the human race, one of the most remarkable is that he designs to consecrate the mouths and tongues of men to his service, making his own voice to be heard in them".[158] There is a great mystery to the preaching of the Gospel which should not be lightly explained away since God himself has deigned to consecrate this instrumentality of humankind. Therefore, we conclude with Calvin "that the glory of God so shines in his Word, that we ought to be so much affected by it, whenever he speaks by his servants, as though he were nigh to us, face to face".[159] The preached word confronts us as that mysterious event in which the persuasive truth of God comes to us through the cordial knowledge of the preacher and his ostensive human word.

The act of preaching the Gospel is Christofocal and therefore Christodynamic. "Christ puts forth his power in the ministry which he has instituted, in such a manner that it is made evident that it was not instituted in vain . . . for he is not separated from the minister, but on the contrary his power is declared efficacious in the minister."[162] On first hearing, those words seem somewhat rash for Calvin could hardly make a more extravagant claim for the wisdom of the preacher's words. But on reflection, we realise that the wisdom to which Calvin is referring resides in the power of Christ himself. As long as Christ remains the Lord and the Master throughout the act of preaching,[163] "Christ through our instrumentality illumines the minds of men, renews their hearts, and in short regenerates them wholly."[164] We could not find more concise language that would be better suited to express the persuasive power of the genuine preacher. All the necessary components are captured in one short sentence. Calvin mentions the illumination of mind, the renewal of the heart, the regeneration of the person, and the instrumentality of the preacher, references which we

K

translate as intellective knowledge, cordial knowledge, persuasive development, and the intellective role of the preacher respectively. Clearly, Calvin believes that our true hearing of the Gospel leads to our persuasive development in Christ. Moreover, Calvin tells us that we can be assured that "nothing that has come out of God's holy mouth can fail in its effect".[165] Even though uttered through the crude and unrefined words of the preacher, "whatever God says in words he fulfils the same in deed; for he speaks that his command immediately becomes his act".[166] Those words are at the same time very hopeful and very disturbing because they tell us the unvarnished truth that the persuasive power of the preached word accomplishes objectively its work within our persons.

Opposing any drift toward subjectivism, and in particular resisting any inclination to reduce preaching to an exclusively internal effect in the heart of the hearer, Calvin insists that "Delirious and even dangerous are those notions, that though the internal word is efficacious, yet that which proceeds from the mouth of man is lifeless and destitute of all power. I indeed admit that the power does not proceed from the tongue of man, nor exists in mere sound, but that the whole power is to be ascribed altogether to the Holy Spirit; there is, however, nothing to hinder the Spirit from putting forth his power in the word preached."[167] Here Calvin is more specific about the power and intelligibility of the preached word. It is the Spirit of Christ who gives the preaching of the Gospel its objective grounding. Also, the ministry of the Spirit arouses a response of faith or a hardening of the heart in the hearer. The persuasive truth of God empowers the human word and the hearer must respond in person. There can be no neutrality in reply to the act of preaching. Calvin states the matter plainly: "The Gospel is never preached in vain, but has invariably an effect, either for life or death."[168] Once more, we cannot fail to appreciate Calvin's foundational themes of the Death and the Resurrection of Jesus Christ. Either the hearer submits freely to the enlivening, transforming act of preaching or else he entrenches further his current, life-sapping ways and he reinforces his established, life-denying, conceptual frame-work. The choice is his alone. Yet there is more mercy in God than sin in us, for "the Gospel has in its own nature a tendency to edification . . . as to its destroying, that comes from something apart from itself — from the fault of mankind".[163] Since, according to Calvin, by man came death through the rejection of the Word of God, we can see why Calvin states that this destroying is a thing apart from the Gospel. If we respond positively to the preaching of the Gospel, then we are spiritually nourished by it and we grow personally, or develop persuasively, in the Second Adam.

Rejoicing that through the persuasive truth of God we obtain salvation and we increase in Christian wisdom, Calvin declares: "The Gospel is not preached that it may only be heard by us, but that it may as a seed of immortal life, altogether reform our hearts."[169] The Gospel has to be implanted before it can germinate and blossom within us. We experience a persuasive development as long as we recognise that listening to the words is not the same thing as hearing the Gospel. We must be willing receivers of the persuasive truth which is clothed in intellective, human words. Nevertheless, the persuasiveness of the truth is independent of the receptiveness of the hearer. The objectivity of this truth means that salvation and edification are conveyed not by the external sound of the voice but by the objective power of the Holy Spirit.[170, 171] In fact, the zeal, the cleverness, and the eloquence of the preacher will accomplish nothing of a spiritual nature unless they are instrumental to this truth. Indeed, because true preaching of the Gospel is a live and efficacious force, many persons who would treat the Gospel like any other truth become the persuaded instruments of God on exposure to it. During the act of preaching and in obedience to Christ, the hearer surrenders willingly all his cherished religious notions, all his presumed knowledge of God and of self, and he accepts humbly the word of another which is directed by the authority of the one Word.

According to Calvin, the Word of God alone is the fountain of our faith, the grounding of our persuasive apprehension, and the reality behind whatever wisdom we have.[172] By this orally declared Word we enter into communion with Christ through faith, and so we share the salvation that he has won for us.[173] Calvin reminds us that faith itself, persuasive apprehension, comes by hearing the Word of God, that is, it comes by the reformation of our persons through the act of preaching.[130] He also says that "God searchingly tests our obedience when we hear his servants not otherwise than if he himself were speaking".[158] Persuasive apprehension is utterly dependent on the act of preaching through which Christ gives his presence in the midst of his Church. By means of this accompanied human word, Christ imparts his grace to persons. Christ establishes his kingdom in their hearts. Calvin is firmly persuaded that the preached word is a means of Christ's self-communication which arouses in us the response of faith. But this channel of grace is only personally effectual through the objective work of the Spirit of Christ. The preached word becomes wisdom for us in so far as it is intellectively oriented by our cordial apprehension of Christ. Even this brief, inadequate outline of Calvin's high valuation of the true preaching of the Gospel provides enough evidence to show that it is intimately related to, indeed inseparable from, his approach to the Word of God. In fact, we can say that, because both are facets of the one mystery that God speaks to humankind, Calvin establishes them on the sure foundation of the Second Adam. And so the doctrine of Scripture makes its presence felt in Calvin's thoughts and words as he seeks to follow the Second Adam and to guide others to a Christofocal appreciation of the act of preaching the Gospel.

In general, we require theological words to do more than convey information if they are to be of service in preaching, teaching, and exposition. Certainly in Calvin's view, they are not meant to communicate a knowledge of themselves. In a fundamental way, they are translucent. At their best, theological words and statements are made in a form most favourable to the reception of their message, although we must not forget that the persuasiveness of that message is

ultimately independent of its reception. The genuine
communicator will always rely on the wisdom of the receiver
for the apprehension of that message. This wisdom involves
attentive listening and obedient responding by the receiver.
Only the act of persuasive apprehension, the event of faith,
can enable the receiver to assimilate the message as he hears
or reads a theological statement. This is also true of course
for the communicating person. We make a theological
statement with the intention of saying something. But this
intention cannot include an anticipation of all that will be
said. By its very nature, an authentic, theological message
points invariably further in certain directions than we can
appreciate. Nevertheless, we do know generally what we
mean to say just before we say it. The nub of the matter is
that the function of wisdom surpasses the knowing of both
what we intend and what we mean. In his original general
discussion, Polanyi declares that "nothing that is said,
written or printed, can ever mean anything in itself; for it is
only a person who utters something — or who listens to it or
reads it — who can mean something by it".[174] Here we have
a key that seems to unlock for us the door to Calvin's great
emphasis on the doctrine of Scripture. Calvin claims
effectively that the Bible does not mean anything in itself; for
it is only the person who utters something from it — or who
listens to it or reads it — who can apprehend what God
means by it. What does God mean by the Scriptures?
Calvin's unambiguous answer to this question is that the
student of Scripture should relate all its parts to the Second
Adam who fulfilled the law of God, to the Person of Jesus
Christ in whom perfect salvation is found. It is not the Bible
that offers life and meaning to fallen humanity. It is Christ
alone who must renew our hearts and illumine our minds
with the doctrine of Scripture. Thus the cordial awareness of
the person grounds all those functions of intending,
meaning, listening, and responding on the reality and
rationality of God. An intellective utterance takes its
bearings from the things of God and of self to which it
points. Its wisdom lies both in the capacity to relate it
correctly to its signified object and in the cordial
apprehension of that object as indicated by that utterance.

CHAPTER 8

BEYOND ATOMISM

PERHAPS the structure of persuasive knowledge appears to some people as an unwarranted theological elaboration of what is spoken and written, of what is spoken and written about, and of the relations between the two. They may think that the coordinated action of cordial-intellective knowing is far too complicated and quite unnecessary to be taken seriously. But, as the twentieth century closes, a tacit appeal to pristine simplicity in biblical studies does not ring true. Indeed, there are vast domains of those studies for which this is manifestly inadequate. Specifically, the widespread use of atomism in contemporary biblical studies is a crude index of their complexity. The fact is that atomism should be of interest to all persons who are in any way concerned with the human mind. By playing a major role in the development of modern science, it has amply demonstrated its worth to the power of human reason in coping with objective aspects of the natural order. Thus it encourages our awareness of its various uses and it emboldens our expectancy of discovering new applications. Since persuasive knowing retains the integrity of human reasoning, and since atomism is a pervasive characteristic of human reasoning, we must set aside all inhibiting, pre-conceived associations of atomism with chance in order to recognise something of the actual, powerful role that atomism already plays in modern biblical studies. Following Calvin's lead, we regard the use of atomistic methods as acceptable provided they are suitably adapted to meet authentic theological requirements. In Calvin's view, scientific methods should never be allowed to eclipse the persuasive truth of the Gospel. They should be subordinated to the primary aim of all genuine biblical studies which is to find Jesus Christ through the guidance of the Holy Spirit. Therefore, atomistic methods should always have intellective biblical applications.

In general, atomism is the reduction of complex entities to unchanging constituent elements. Linguistic atomism with its use of the alphabet is the most common form, although relatively few people probably realise that the simple act of spelling a word is an application of atomism. Logical atomism is also familiar to many people who were first acquainted with the fundamental propositions of the Euclidean geometry at school. Even biological atomism is fairly well known through popular accounts of the scientific investigations of cells and genes. Undoubtedly, foremost in the popular mind of this nuclear age is the atomism of chemistry and physics. Probably the least familiar form is literary atomism which none the less has much in common with the atomism of modern chemistry. In particular, the latter has shown that atomic methods can be applied successfully even where the basic units are not isolable species randomly distributed but components in an ordered system. Correspondingly, ancient literature is often rewardingly regarded as the art of arranging components in an ordered system. Moreover, atomism is frequently presupposed or tacitly acknowledged in modern science, for example, in the application of group theory to symmetrical molecules and to ordered crystals. Studies of molecular structures are considerably simplified by the determination and the use of the molecular point group. Similarly, investigations of crystal structures are markedly eased by the determination and the use of the space group of the crystalline solid. But literary atomism cannot benefit from the same extensive indistinguishability either of its fundamental units or of their modes of combination. Nevertheless, countless researches on ancient literature, including biblical studies, depend on procedures that are formally analogous to the atomic methods of modern chemistry and physics. Biblical atomism is perhaps most obvious in form criticism. For the sake of simplicity we limit our present remarks to the synoptic Gospels. In places the Gospel according to Mark comprises a number of incidents and sayings that are simply and obviously joined together and that can be readily isolated. This becomes even more apparent where the Gospels of Matthew and Luke are arranged in synopsis with Mark. Then the same literary unit often appears in different contexts. In atomistic terms, we can say that the Gospels contain isolable, unchanging, constituent elements. And so the easy distinguishability of one literary section from another allows a useful procedure of criticism. Those units are first isolated from their ordered systems or Gospels and then they are categorised according to their individual forms, thus closely paralleling the group theoretic methods of chemistry and physics.

This reduction of complexity to basic units is of course an analytical procedure. Being the only available critical strategy for the systematic, intellectual exploration of the complexities of life and nature, it appeals strongly to the human mind as the predominant, unaided, intellectual method of investigation. In fact, all Christians use reduction in one form or another when reading the Scriptures. As we have already stated, even the biblical mechanic uses it unwittingly. In its most developed form, literary atomism proceeds in a stepwise fashion from one isolable unit to the next. The difficulty of each step depends on the discreteness and permanence of the identified units that are categorised in the attempt to simplify the critical study. The members of each category or set are then treated in some way as intrinsically equivalent units, even if only to isolate the variations on a common content. Clearly, this method gives discontinuity logical priority over all notions of continuity. Indeed, this is the powerful insight which lies behind the great success of perturbation theory in natural science. In effect, biblical criticism presupposes that the observed variations of the one discrete unit result from minor perturbations of that unit by the Gospel contexts. Thus the critical intellect pays attention to and thinks about the discrete units before it attends to the linkages between them. This assumed functional priority of substantive units could possibly have been the pre-eminent criterion of the original selection of material during the composition of the Gospels, but that is very difficult to establish. Even if this can be established, it does not automatically follow that the same priority must continue to hold after the formation of the Gospel. The very act of integration transforms invariably the meanings of the individual units. In principle, there is nothing to prevent such a transformation imparting new meaning to a literary unit, in which case the Gospel context would produce more than a minor perturbation. Besides, the treatment of the discrete units as discontinuous entities demands the same handling for the linkages. Consequently, the investigation of the corresponding, discontinuous, linking processes requires the further use of atomistic methods.

Critical biblical scholarship reduces the complexity of the Gospels by the predominantly analytical procedures of textual, source, and form criticism. Also, the discreteness and the permanence of the literary units are regularly attributed to ancient oral traditions or earlier literary sources. In addition, those units are categorised as pronouncement stories, miracle stories, sayings of Jesus *etc.*, and their forms and their contents are investigated, usually in isolation from the text. With the critical intellect attending to and thinking about the formal units prior to contextual considerations, hypothetical origins are inevitably advanced and awareness of the real context is blunted. We can say that the tendency is to regard the literary units as exclusively descriptive and demonstrative rather than intellective. In other words, human reason is often tacitly idolised in the reductive form of biblical atomism. Also, the persuasive truth of the Gospel is eclipsed as the doctrine of the Scripture is ignored or even denied. Yet the plain fact is that atomism is much more than merely logical analysis. For example, its basic assumption is that there is a limit to division. Atomism assumes that small ultimate units exist and that large scale complexes are to be accounted for in terms of those ultimate units. This is the essence of biblical atomism. Only a perverse mind would refuse to concede willingly that its underlying assumption carries the biblical scholar a great distance along the critical trail. A survey of the evidence for the discrete nature of a kaleidoscopic diversity of portions of Scripture would cover a vast and rapidly expanding literature. But, as our study of Calvin's theology emphasises, data of this kind cannot prove that the component, structures exclusively determine the real meaning or true purpose of a particular passage. The available data may point unmistakably to the discreteness of earlier forms of the biblical literature but that tells us nothing about things like the ministry of the Holy Spirit, persuasive knowing, and the doctrine of Scripture. A powerful psychological appeal is at work here. The limited, critical task of isolating ultimate units appears to promise considerably high rewards. Having discovered the supposedly earlier functions of those basic units, interpretation of the Gospel combinations readily follows, or so it seems. Apparently, all that is required is an integration of those discovered functions.

But isn't this analytic approach to the Scriptures a perversion and a sacrilege? Isn't it an arrogant assault on the Bible, an attempt to reduce the sacred to the profane? Are we not tearing the Scriptures to pieces instead of accepting, enjoying, and using them as they are? The literalists are not alone in their concern for the order, harmony, and purpose of the Scriptures as an unique whole. Many persons who reject both literalism and liberalism question with good reason the neglect of aspects of the Bible which mark and integrate its contents. Atomism certainly disrupts this unity as it studies isolated parts. By its very nature, it does so before proceeding to the task of attending to the ordering relations of the units of the received biblical composition. Biblical atomism is therefore the study of structure and that structure includes the relations of parts regarded as forms of atomistic ordering. By placing less emphasis on the hypothetical functions of the literary units and concentrating more on the knowable structures of the various relations among them, a greater reliance on context can be advantageously developed. This is not a trivial suggestion although it too can rely solely on human reasoning. It is well known that in many cases isolated particulars are not recognised as parts of a comprehensive entity. Even where they are, they take on an entirely new meaning. Hence, in biblical studies, the interplay of a knowledge of the form and the content of the literary units with that of their orderings can markedly increase the possible interpretations of both units and orderings by drawing previously concealed features out into the light of reason. But, as we have already noted, interpretation is not the same thing as meaning. According to the theology of Calvin, what gives real meaning to an interpretation is its grounding on the reality of Jesus Christ. Thus the discernment of this interplay should result from a persuasive apprehension of the Scriptures which regards both the literary units and their relational orderings as intellective knowledge oriented by a cordial knowledge of the doctrine of Scripture. In other words, while our critical, atomistic methods usefully identify the basic units, our persuasive apprehension ensures that we also appreciate that those units and their orderings point beyond themselves to the invariant, eternal doctrine of the Scripture.

Once more, modern science provides us with a powerful illustration of the great significance of this kind of systematic two-way interplay. The view that stable particles or atoms are the ultimate bases of natural phenomena is now rejected by physicists. Such a view no longer fits the facts, and so today we hear that all matter in the universe consists of particles of the families of leptons and quarks. Three pairs of lepton, including the electron and its elusive neutrino, make up the 'light stuff' of the universe and six kinds of quarks are known to constitute the 'heavy stuff' of the universe. The quarks have distinctive 'flavours' or properties. In fact, their fanciful names of 'up', 'down', 'charm', 'strange', 'top', and 'bottom' reflect these exotic properties which are vaguely akin to, but distinct from, the more familiar 'positive' and 'negative' electric charges. While physicists still lack the experimental evidence to substantiate to their own satisfaction their concepts of a Grand Unified Field Theory, they now talk freely of unisolable, fundamental particles. Thus what used to be regarded as an independent, permanent substance or mode of existence — a material particle — has been discovered to be a complex of inter-changing entities in a changing environment. In short, the attempted isolation of basic units with unchanging properties has failed in physics at the most fundamental levels.

Much the same can be said of the fundamental units of biblical criticism. Biblical students should learn from physics that the patterns of changing relations have also to be reduced to order before a real grasp of the Gospel can be obtained. This suggests that two important aspects should be taken into account in biblical studies: first, the wider context of a literary unit should be carefully considered and secondly, a keen sensitivity to patterns of changing factors should be cultivated. Of course, human reasoning alone cannot hope to transform interpretation into meaningful-ness. Only persuasive knowing can attain that goal. That is what modern physics can teach biblical scholars, if they do not already know it. And even if we do, it still calls our attention to a pervasive deficiency in biblical scholarship. We need to recognise the tremendous importance of the obvious fact that literary units change in meaning and in purpose as they are incorporated within the Gospel narrative. Only by doing this, can we hope to follow Calvin's economic treatment of passages with his intellective use of critical reflection and his reliance on cordial knowledge of the doctrine of Scripture. Without the guidance of the Holy Spirit, our acute concern for the context and the purpose of the passage, phrase, or word will never carry us beyond interpretation and we will not reach real meaning anchored in the invariant doctrine of Scripture.

By and large, the facts of biblical criticism are recognised and isolated by experts who display a definite skill and a definite urge to simplify the accounts of the biblical contents. Unless we are prepared to assert that those scholars are totally bereft of the gift of the Holy Spirit, we can safely assume with Calvin that both the urge and the execution of their art are at least partly based on experience which cannot be specified in terms of explicit rules. The fact that many scholars neither specify nor take into account this kind of experience does not mean that they do not benefit from it. The essential points are that even biblical criticism relies on something other than exclusively critical knowledge and that the Holy Spirit may still work through the imperfect instrument of biblical criticism. The fact remains, however, that only when the persuasive truth of the Gospel is responded to humbly and obediently, does cordial knowledge orient and sustain the integrated openness of intellective knowledge. If the latter is reduced without remainder to explicit, critical knowledge, it is simultaneously dissociated from the only source of integration, namely, the Holy Spirit. The critical scholar is therefore confronted by his own atomisation of the biblical contents. Having denied himself access to the only valid integration of the biblical material, the critical scholar resorts to the human alternative. He produces his own involuted, imaginative synthesis. We require to replace urgently second hand biblical scholarship that discusses other people's God and someone else's Jesus with Christian wisdom grounded on first hand experience of the persuasive truth. We need a persuasive development of biblical studies on which to base our modern preaching, teaching, and theology. Can we possibly find a better way to start than with *The Institutes* which, according to Calvin, was tailor-made for this job?

We may well ask at this point: are we not devaluing the powers of human speech and of the written word? The immense, intellectual superiority of humankind over animals has been attributed almost entirely to the gift of speech.[175] If the power of cordial knowing predominates in the domain of explicitly formulated Christian knowledge, can we still credit our capacity to use language with such tremendous intellectual advantages? A comprehensive answer to this question would have to discuss the relation between persuasive knowing and human intelligence throughout the entire range of Calvin's work; it can be given here only in very brief and incomplete outline. We offer a

Polanyian acount suitably modified in the light of Calvin's theology. As Polanyi notes, language offers the obvious advantage of verbal communication.[175] Many theological scholars would argue that we profit by information received through the communications of our spiritual forebears, especially by the contributions of the Early Church fathers and the reformers, communications that have been transmitted cumulatively from one generation to the next. But articulation does not merely make us better informed. It can enrich us even more by functioning as an aid to the development of our persuasive knowledge of any given piece of information. Our cordial knowledge and our intellective knowledge may be developed as articulation provides signs for us along the narrow Christian way. Our spirituality is nourished as the Holy Spirit works through the instrumentality of the condensed activity of others. For example, in so far as letters, treatises, and biblical commentaries direct us to Christ through the Word of God, they offer wonderful opportunities for the expansion and the reorientation of our intellective knowledge from ever new cordial points of departure. And each opportunity promises a persuasive experience similar to the personal event which redeems and reconciles us to God. This kind of experience, therefore, gains a greater dominion over our lives for it is part of that profound recognition by which the Christian can continue to grow personally in the love and grace of Jesus Christ.

Like Polanyi, "we can explain the tremendous intellectual advantages of articulation",[176] but unlike Polanyi, we can do it without in the least ignoring or submerging the supremacy of the Christian's persuasive powers. Although the intellectual superiority of humankind over the animals remains its use of signs, this utilisation itself is now seen to be a cordial, supracritical process, or in plain words, a spiritual activity. The accumulation and the reconsideration of various subject matters in terms of the signs indicating them are oriented and integrated by our inarticulate, cordial power. This is an activity involving wisdom, and as such it can occur only within our persons, not through the manipulation of symbols on paper or even in the mind. Our whole articulate apparatus turns out to be a supremely effective medium for the transmission of the power of our inarticulate spiritual faculties in keeping with Calvin's view of the Scriptures as the unique medium for the deposit of the doctrine of Scripture. So we begin to fathom Calvin's depth of insight in his concern for the invariant doctrine of Scripture rather than for literalist inerrancy. We conclude therefore that the cordial component of Christian knowledge predominates also in the domain of explicit knowledge. At all levels it is the Christian's ultimate faculty for receiving and holding knowledge of God and of self.

Conscious of our deep indebtedness to Calvin, Einstein, and Polanyi for our apprehension of the nature of persuasive knowledge, we may now face effectively the problem raised in the opening sentences of this essay by the supracritical character of cordial knowledge. We have indicated that when we grow in wisdom, when our intellective knowledge is reoriented, or when we relate a critical statement and the facts to which it refers, our cordial power is at work in the assimilation of a greater knowledge of God and of self. We are prompted to clarify, to amplify, or to rectify something said or experienced. We are directed away from an apprehension that no longer commands from us a proper conviction to another which we find more compelling. And this is how the Truth draws us ever closer to himself and how he empowers us to hold pieces of information only in so far as they point us to himself. Here is the persuasive experience of our own of which we wrote at the beginning of this essay. It is the necessary act of personal participation in our explicit knowledge of the things of God and of self, an act that we can be aware of and know in an unreflecting manner. And this situation now no longer appears as a rational oddity for it seems that the kind of cordial power by which we are committed to any particular statement operates in various forms throughout the domain of Christian knowledge. Also, we have seen that it is this personal component alone that endows our intellective statements with meaning and conviction. All Christian knowledge is now known to be shaped and sustained through the inarticulate, suprarational faculty which we share in Christ, in whom we find our true selves or persons.

This modern expression of Calvin's theology in suitably adapted Einsteinian and Polanyian terms entails a decisive change in our notion of Christian knowledge. The participation of the knower in the shaping of his knowledge, which has been tolerated by many scholars only as a flaw in biblical and theological studies is now recognised as the hallmark of reforming, theological cognition. It is not a shortcoming to be eliminated from critical knowledge but rather the sign and seal that critical knowledge is truly instrumental to Christian knowing. We acknowledge now that our powers of knowing can operate without causing us to make any explicit statements; and that, even when we do make them, they serve as pointers for extending the range of the persuasive knowledge that originated them. Since the ideal of a knowledge embodied in strictly impersonal statements now appears self-contradictory and meaningless, we must learn to accept as paramount in the study of the Bible and of theology a knowledge of God and of self that is manifestly personal. Such a position appears difficult; for what we seem to be referring to as knowledge is something that we could apparently determine at will, as the mood takes us. Yet persuasive knowledge is fully determined because it can be pursued only with utter commitment to Christ and, therefore, to the invariant doctrine of Scripture. When guided by the Holy Spirit and the Word of God, our capacity and passion to know the rationality and the reality of God in Christ will always ensure that our personal judgment will achieve the full measure of truth that meets the requirements of our particular Christian calling.

Throughout our discussion we have drawn freely on scientific knowledge to assist our apprehension of persuasive knowledge. In fact, we have seen how Calvin safeguards the open structure of persuasive knowledge, thus allowing us to benefit from modern science. Within a single variable conception of knowing, Calvin comprises the process of assimilating knowledge of God, of self, and of the universe.

Though our outline is sketchy, it suggests an approach to Christian knowing that reveals the essential unity of Christian theology and modern science. The structure of persuasive knowing is manifested most clearly in the growth of wisdom. It is a process of apprehending; a personal responding, through the Holy Spirit employing explicit instruments, to the inexpressible intention of seeking Jesus Christ. Recognising that personal participation characterises cordial-intellective knowledge, we now indicate aspects of Christian knowing that are decisive for our understanding of wisdom and modern science. In Christian knowing, we always respond through the Holy Spirit and through the instruments of the Word of God to their intention, Jesus Christ. By instruments of the Word of God we mean our limited, intellective knowledge of the Scriptures. We cannot comprehend the fulness of Christ or the totality of the doctrine of Scripture but we may successively advance from a wisdom of one set of instruments to the developed wisdom of a set of improved instruments. This means that we come to know progressively more and more of the Word surpassing words. This expanding wisdom cannot be effortless on our part for it requires our teachable receiving and our obedient serving of the disclosures of divine reality. The same faculty of wisdom is at work in all Christian knowing which is not a passive process but a personal experience. Yet wisdom is not irreversibly established since at any stage in our persuasive development we are prone to lose it by denying its proper use. By looking at the several instruments of a particular stage of development rather than through those instruments, we may succeed in diverting our attention away from the pursuit of our primary intention and we may even lose sight of Jesus Christ altogether.

According to Einstein or Polanyi, scientific knowing is a sympathetic process of apprehending; a personal responding to the inexpressible intention of researching the rationality of the universe. This responding occurs through an intuitive relation to reality that employs explicit instruments. In short, Einstein's sympathetic knowledge, Polanyi's personal knowledge, and Calvin's persuasive knowledge share the

same formal structure. Since the working scientist has
neither need nor occasion to refer to the activity either of the
intuitive relation or of the Holy Spirit in the reports of his
researches, the scientific contributions of the Christian and
the non-Christian will be indistinguishable in form and in
content. Moreover, in scientific knowing, we always
respond through the intuitive relation or the Holy Spirit and
through the instruments of scientific theories and
experiments to their intention, the rationality of the
universe. Those instruments are our limited, intellective
knowledge of the laws of nature. We cannot comprehend the
completeness of the rationality of the universe or the entirety
of the laws of nature but we may successively advance from a
wisdom of one set of instruments or theories and
experiments to the developed wisdom of a set of improved
instruments. This means that we come to know
progressively more and more of the rationality surpassing
our rationalities. And so we could continue to unfold the
parallelism between persuasive knowing and scientific
knowing, bearing in mind that this formal similarity is
effectively a practical equivalence in scientific research.

  Those considerations can be transposed into the elements
of an open account of Christian knowledge. Following
Calvin,[177] we can say that, when we are led by the Holy
Spirit to apprehend a particular set of instruments as serving
their intention, our critical awareness has been focused
through their previously unrecognised signalities on their
joint meaning. This focal point of attention does not make us
unaware of the signs, since we are led to appreciate an
intention only through its instruments, but it changes
altogether the manner in which we are made aware of the
instruments.[178] We are made aware of them now in terms of
the intention on which our attention has been fixed. We call
this an instrumental awareness of the signs by contrast with
an intentional awareness which would fix our attention on
these signs themselves and not as instruments of the
intention. We also speak correspondingly of an instrumental
knowledge of such signs, as distinct from an intentional
knowledge of the same individual signs and we now

illustrate this distinction. In general, biblical or theological words and statements are never objects of our attention in themselves. They are pointers towards the things to which they refer. If our attention is shifted from the meaning of a word to that word as an object viewed in itself, its meaning for us is temporarily destroyed.[178] Similarly, if we divert our concentration from the meaning of a biblical passage to that passage as an object viewed in itself, its meaning is temporarily destroyed. Words serve as instruments of meaning only by being known instrumentally while fixing our intentional attention on their meaning. Biblical passages serve as instruments of meaning only by being known instrumentally while fixing our intentional attention on their meaning. And this is similarly true of words used in worship including praise, prayer, and preaching. Their meaning lies in their purpose; they do not lead to prayer, praise, and preaching, when observed as objects in themselves, but only when used instrumentally by fixing our intentional attention on their purpose. The use of words in prayer, for example, can be paralysed by listening to their recitation instead of attending to their purpose. Likewise, the use of words in both praise and preaching can be abrogated by attending to their eloquence and artistry.

This brings out the essential point where Calvin parts company with Einstein and Polanyi. Words and statements in theology and worship are for us sacred instruments only in so far as they are instrumentally experienced as an expression of the Person of Jesus Christ within us. And we must realise then that our own person has a special place in the world; we never attend to our true self as an object in itself. Our own person serves as a basic instrument of Christ in as much as we are intentionally responding to God's will in and for our situation. Hence in all our obedient moments, we are instrumentally aware of our person within our intentional knowledge of God's will for the world about us. To be aware of our person, of our true self in Christ, in terms of the things we know and do, is to feel spiritually alive.[179] This awareness is an essential part of our existence as wise, practical persons. But we can recognise this sacred instrumentality also in other forms of awareness. Every time a new instrument is assimilated to Christ through the Holy Spirit in our person, Christ finds new expression within us as we are expanded into fresh modes of being and service. We indicated earlier that the whole realm of Christian wisdom relies on the use of language. We can reformulate this now by stating that all spiritual life by which we surpass the animals springs from within us as the articulate framework of Christian teaching is instrumentally experienced as an expression of the Person of Jesus Christ. The vast accumulation of explicit, theological statements and the systematisations of those statements by Christian theologians throughout the ages can also be experienced as an equally extensive expression of the Person of Christ within us. Instrumental awareness is like a temporary dwelling of the Person of Jesus Christ within the subject of which we are instrumentally aware. An articulate framework is used like a tent by our wisdom; it is a resting place for wisdom along the open way of life and growth, so to speak, one more sojourn that satisfies further our hunger for clarity of purpose.

All kinds of Christian knowing involve a personal participation of the knower in the instrumental details known by him as pointing to their joint meaning or purpose. Only a totally isolated and completely meaningless instrument, like a word or perhaps a sentence, could be brought fully to our intentional attention, but even in this case, we are instrumentally aware of our personal readjustments in terms of the supposed nature of the object in question. Since apprehension can be destroyed altogether by shifting attention from its intention to its instrumental signs, it is not surprising to find that we often apprehend intentions without ever having intentionally attended to their signs. Indeed, biblical literalism and liberalism benefit from, but refuse to acknowledge, this ability. In such cases we are intentionally ignorant of those signs; we know them only instrumentally in terms of what they jointly mean, but we cannot tell what they are in themselves. The scientist's intuitive insights and the biblical student's knowledge of the doctrine of Scripture are experiences involving kinds of knowledge that can never be told. In general, signs that are not known intentionally are unspecifiable, and there are vast domains of knowledge relating to Christian living, the pointers to which are largely unspecifiable. The personal capacities of faith, hope, and love are preeminent. We know, for example, that we are in love without being able to tell, except vaguely, by what signs we recognise it. And this is also how the other person is known. A person can be known only instrumentally, that is, by experiencing the unspecifiable signs of his person as an expression of the Person of Christ in terms of an intentional knowledge of God's love for him.

This conception of a person allows us to attribute to another person the same faculties of wisdom which we use in apprehending him. For the unspecifiable signs of his person, through which we experience an expression of the Person of Christ, are that person's own signs. They are the personal actions of which he himself is instrumentally aware in terms of his intentional knowledge of God's will for the world. Indeed we ourselves, meeting the person, are part of that world. He and we may be mutually apprehending each other by experiencing one another's unspecifiable, personal signs. In more familiar words, we may be loving our neighbour as ourselves. Thus we have a continuous transition from the personal knowing of things to the personal meeting and intercourse between Christians. We regard this as a substantial advance towards that unifying perspective of the different aspects of the Christian which we set out to sketch.

We attend now to some features of wisdom which we have only hinted at so far. We have referred to our hunger for clarity of purpose and we have assumed the presence of a humble teachableness. Both keep us open to ever closer contact with the reality and rationality of God in Jesus Christ. These are powerful forces for pursuing the highest hope of the Christian. Indeed, if the shaping of knowledge is achieved through our experiencing new forms of existence, the assimilation of knowledge should be found to be motivated by the deepest forces sustaining our being. As for the creature, Polanyi aptly comments, "we see, in fact, that repeated frustrations in solving a harassing problem can destroy the problem-solver's emotional balance — even if he is an animal".[180] In the case of the Christian, we can say that his whole person, that is, his complete range of feelings, his entire reach of intelligence, and his full scope of spirit, is enlivened by the Holy Spirit through his articulate heritage as tested by the Word of God. Every increment of this edifying experience is prompted by the Holy Spirit, served by the Word of God, and accompanied by an expression of the Person of Jesus Christ within the Christian. To someone on the alert for God in Christ, therefore, whatever seems offensive intimates a need and it stirs him to the prospect of divine disclosure. Thus the active Christian will avail himself of ever new opportunities to undergo a change that will make his instrumental life more enriching for all around him, including his growing self in Christ.

Finally, the word disclosure carries connotations that recall the notion of wisdom as a search for a hidden reality. But only something that is already there can disclose itself. The Christian cannot seek to experience a disclosure of anything unless he is convinced that it is there, ready to reveal itself. The recognition of this hidden presence is in fact half the battle: it means that the Christian has encountered a real need and is asking the right questions. In this situation as he turns to the Word of God, he is like the little boy who asks the carver to whittle away the wood from around the figure that the craftsman perceives inside the piece of oak. Here then is a very brief answer to the important question: whether knowledge, admittedly shaped through the knower, can be determined by him as he thinks fit? A commited search for the correct answer to a particular need leaves no arbitrary choice open to the seeker. He will not have to guess, but he must make the utmost effort to search properly. The sense of the pre-existent answer in Jesus Christ makes the shaping of knowledge a responsible act, free from subjective predilections. And it endows by the same token the results of such acts with a claim to universal validity. For when you believe that a hidden reality reveals the answer to your personal needs, you will expect it to be equally recognisable, though not necessarily recognised, by other Christians. To accept persuasive knowledge as valid is to accept such claims as justified, while acknowledging gratefully the limitations imposed graciously by the particular talents. This opportunity is then regarded as the Christian's calling — the calling which determines his responsibilities, whether in modern science, in Christian theology, or in both, in the pursuit of knowledge of God and of self.

REFERENCES

1. John Calvin, *The Institutes Of The Christian Religion,* translated by Ford Lewis Battles, Philadelphia: The Westminster Press, 1960. [*The Institutes*]
2. *The Institutes,* 1559 Introduction.
3. *Ibid.,* I.13.3.
4. *Ibid.,* I.1.1.
5. *Ibid.,* I.1.1-2.
6. Michael Polanyi, *The Study Of Man,* Chicago: The University of Chicago Press, 1958, p. 11.
7. *Ibid.,* p. 12.
8. *The Institutes,* I.5.1.
9. *Ibid.,* II.8.17.
10. *Ibid.,* I.6.
11. *Ibid.,* I.7.5.
12. *Ibid.,* I.7.4.
13 Albert Einstein, *Ideas and Opinions,* translated by Sonja Bargmann, London: Souvenir Press Ltd., 1973, p. 271.
14. Iain Paul, *Science, Theology, and Einstein,* Belfast: Christian Journals Ltd., 1982, p. 33.
15. *Ideas and Opinions,* p. 266.
16. *Science, Theology, and Einstein,* pp. 43-50.
17. *The Institutes,* I.8.13.
18. *Ibid.,* III.2.7.
19. *Ibid.,* III.2.6.
20. *Ibid.,* III.2.14.
21. *Ibid.,* III.1.4.
22. Michael Polanyi, *Personal Knowledge: Towards a Post-Critical Philosophy,* London: Routledge & Kegan Paul Ltd., 1969, p. vii.
23. *Ibid.,* pp. 10-11.
24. *Ibid.,* p. 13.
25. *Ibid.,* p. 5.
26. Michael Polanyi, *The Tacit Dimension,* London: Routledge & Kegan Paul Ltd., 1967, p. 4.
27. *Ibid.,* p. 7.
28. *The Institutes,* IV.8.5.
29. *Ibid.,* IV.8.8.
30. Colossians, 1:15.

31. John Calvin, *Commentary on Hebrews*, translated by John Owen, Grand Rapids, Michigan: Baker Book House, 1979, p. 271. [Heb. 11:6].
32. *The Institutes*, III.19.4.
33. *Ibid.*, III.8.4.
34. *Ibid.*, III.7.10.
35. Michael Polanyi, *Science, Faith, and Society*, Chicago: The University of Chicago Press, 1979, p. 24.
36. *The Institutes*, II.7.15.
37. *Ibid.*, IV.20.15.
38. *Ibid.*, III.19.7.
39. T. F. Torrance, *Theology in Reconstruction*, London: SCM Press Ltd., 1965, p. 20.
40. *The Study of Man*, pp. 12-13.
41. *The Institutes*, III.2.13-14.
42. *Theology in Reconstruction*, p. 28.
43. John Murray, *Calvin on Scripture and Divine Sovereignty*, London: Evangelical Press, 1979 [see footnote p. 16]. [Murray]
44. *The Institutes*, I.6.3.
45. *Ibid.*, I.7.1 [Murray, pp. 16-17].
46. *Ibid.*, I.7.5 [Murray, p. 16].
47. Murray, pp. 17-18, *Calvin's Comm.*, II Timothy 3:16.
48. Murray, p. 18, *Calvin's Comm.*, II Peter 1:20.
49. Murray, pp. 18-19, *Calvin's Comm. The Argument on the Gospel of Jesus Christ: According to Matthew, Mark, and Luke.*
50. Murray, p. 19, *Calvin's Comm. The Argument to the Gospel of John.*
51. Murray, p. 19, *Calvin's Comm.*, Romans 15:4.
52. Murray, p. 22, *Calvin's Comm.*, Ephesians 2:5.
53. Murray, p. 22.
54. Murray, p. 22, *Calvin's Comm.*, Hebrews 9:1.
55. Murray, pp. 22-23, *Calvin's Comm.*, 1 Timothy 1:3.
56. Murray, p. 23, *Calvin's Comm.*, James 4:7.
57. Murray, p. 23.
58. Murray, p. 25.
59. Murray, p. 25, *Calvin's Comm.*, Romans 10:6.
60. Murray, p. 25, *Calvin's Comm.*, Romans 11:8.
61. Murray, p. 25, *Calvin's Comm.*, Ephesians 4:8.
62. Murray, p. 12.
63. Murray, p. 29, *Calvin's Comm.*, *Harm. Evang.*, Matthew 27:9.
64. Murray, p. 29, *Calvin's Comm.*, Acts 7:14.
65. Murray, p. 29, *Calvin's Comm.*, Acts 7:16.
66. Murray, pp. 29-31, *Calvin's Comm.*, Hebrews 11:21.
67. C. A. Coulson & A. Jeffrey, *Waves: A mathematical approach to the common types of wave motion*, London: Longman Group Ltd., 1977.
68. John Cunningham, *Towards Quantum Mechanics*, London: Transworld Publishers Ltd., 1972, pp. 11-12.

69. G. J. Whitrow, *Philosophical Journal*, 14, p. 70 (1977).

70. Albert Einstein, *Relativity, The Special and General Theories*, translated by R. W. Lawson, Whitstable: Latimer Trend, 1960.

71. Hermann Bondi, *Assumption and Myth in Physical Theory*, Cambridge: Cambridge University Press, 1967, p. 4.

72. D. R. Hofstadter, *Gödel, Escher, Bach: An Eternal Golden Braid*, Harmondsworth: Penguin Books Ltd., 1983, p. 88.

73. Lawrence Sklar, *Space, Time, and Spacetime*, Berkeley and Los Angeles: University of California Press, 1977, p. 14.

74. *Ibid.*, pp. 14-15.

75. *Gödel, Escher, Bach*, p. 91.

76. *Study of Man*, p. 15.

77. *The Institutes*, I.8.1.

78. John Calvin, *Commentary on the Book of Psalms*, translated by James Anderson, Grand Rapids, Michigan: Baker Book House, 1979, Volume First, p. xl.

79. *The Institutes*, I.8.2.

80. *Ibid.*, I.8.11.

81. John Calvin, *Commentaries on the Second Epistle to Timothy*, translated by William Pringle, Grand Rapids, Michigan: Baker Book House, 1979, pp. 246-51 [II Timothy 3: 14-16].

82. *The Institutes*, I.7.2.

83. *Ibid.*, I.14.4.

84. John Calvin, *Commentaries on the Epistle of Paul to the Galatians*, translated by William Pringle, Grand Rapids, Michigan: Baker Book House, 1979, p. 136 [Galatians 4:22].

85. *The Institutes*, IV.16.23.

86. *Ibid.*, IV.17.23.

87. *Ibid.*, II.8.8.

88. *Commentary on Hebrews*, p. 36 [1:3].

89. *The Institutes*, II.8.26.

90. *Ibid.*, I.6.1.

91. *Gödel, Escher, Bach*, p. 20.

92. *Ibid.*, p. 21.

93. *Ibid.*, p. 24.

94. *Ibid.*, p. 18.

95. *Ibid.*, p. 19.

96. *Personal Kowledge*, p. 95.

97. *The Institutes*, I.15.3.

98. *Ibid.*, I.15.4.

99. *Ibid.*, I.2.1.

100. *Ibid.*, I.5.11.

101. *Ibid.*, I.14.21.

102. *Ibid.*, II.2.12.

103. *Ibid.*, II.1.4.

104. *Goedel, Escher, Bach*, p. 56.

105. *Ideas and Opinions,* p. 262.
106. *Ibid.,* p. 47.
107. *Ibid.,* p. 42.
108. *Science, Theology, and Einstein,* p. 43.
109. *Ideas and Opinions,* p. 226.
110. *Personal Knowledge,* pp. 9-15.
111. Albert Einstein, *Annalen der Physik, 17,* 891 (1905).
112. A. A. Michelson & E. W. Morley, *American Journal of Science, 34,* 333 (1887).
113. Albert Einstein, *Autobiographical Notes* in *Albert Einstein: Philosopher-Scientist,* edited by P. A. Schilpp, New York: Tudor Publishing Company, 1951, p. 53.
114. *Personal Knowledge,* p. 11 [footnote].
115. *Ibid.,* p. 12.
116. D. C. Miller, *Proceedings of the National Academy of Science, 9,* 306 (1925) [see *Personal Knowledge,* pp. 12-14].
117. *Theology in Reconstruction,* p. 29.
118. *The Institutes,* II.2.15.
119. *Ibid.,* II.2.4.
120. *Ibid.,* II.2.18.
121. *Ibid.,* II.2.16.
122. John Calvin, *Commentaries on the First Book of Moses called Genesis,* translated by John King, Grand Rapids, Michigan: Baker Book House, 1979, pp. 85ff. [Genesis 1:15].
123. *Ibid.,* p. 86 [Genesis 1:16].
124. Philip Kitcher, *Abusing Science: The Case Against Creationism,* Milton Keynes: Open University Press, 1982.
125. Steven Weinberg, *The First Three Minutes: A Modern View of the Universe,* London: Fontana Paperbacks, 1983.
126. L. E. Orgel, *The Origins of Life: Molecules and Natural Selection,* London: Chapman and Hall Ltd., 1973.
127. Ilya Prigogine, *From Being to Becoming: Time and Complexity in the Physical Sciences,* San Francisco: W. H. Freeman and Company, 1980.
128. *The Study of Man,* p. 17.
129. *Ibid.,* p. 18.
130. *The Institutes,* II.2.11; IV.17.25.
131. *Ibid.,* II.15.
132. *Ibid.,* III.1.1.
133. *Ibid.,* III.1.4.
134. *Ibid.,* III.11.5.
135. C. W. Kilmister, *Special Theory of Relativity,* Oxford: Pergamon Press Ltd., 1970, pp. 187-8.
136. *Ibid.,* p. 145.
137. H. A. Lorentz, A. Einstein, H. Minkowski and H. Weyl, *The Principle Of Relativity,* translated by W. Perrett and G. B. Jeffrey, New York: Dover Publications, Inc., 1952, p. 83.

138. C. W. Kilmister, *General Theory of Relativity,* Oxford: Pergamon Press Ltd., 1973, p. 58.
139. *Ibid.,* p. 60.
140. *The First Three Minutes,* pp. 104ff.
141. *The Institutes,* II.7.3.
142. *Ibid.,* IV.13.13.
143. *Ibid.,* II.8.59.
144. *Ibid.,* III.7.1.
145. *Ibid.,* II.8.7.
146. Matthew 5:5.
147. *The Institutes,* III.3.9.
148. *Science, Theology, and Einstein,* pp. 121-5.
149. *The Institutes,* III.3.8.
150. *Ibid.,* III.3.10.
151. *Ibid.,* III.11.1.
152. *The Study of Man,* p. 20.
153. *The Institutes,* I.13.14.
154. *Science, Theology, and Einstein,* pp. 55f.
155. *The Institutes,* IV.14.26.
156. *Ibid.,* IV.1.9.
157. John Calvin, *Commentary on the Book of the Prophet Isaiah,* translated by William Pringle, Grand Rapids, Michigan: Baker Book House, 1979, Volume Fourth, p. 172 [Isaiah 55:11].
158. *The Institutes,* IV.1.5.
159. John Calvin, *The Commentaries of John Calvin on the Prophet Haggai,* translated by John Owen, Grand Rapids, Michigan: Baker Book House, 1979, p. 341 [Haggai 1:12].
160. John Calvin, *Commentaries on Isaiah,* p. 61 [Isaiah 50:10].
161. John Calvin, *Commentary on Matthew,* Volume Second, p. 121 [Matthew 13:37].
162. John Calvin, *Commentary on the Epistles of Paul the Apostle to the Corinthians,* translated by John Pringle, Grand Rapids, Michigan: Baker Book House, 1979, Volume First, p. 129 [I Corinthians 3:7].
163. John Calvin, *Commentary on Corinthians,* Volume Second, p. 329 [II Corinthians 10:8].
164. *Ibid.,* Volume Second, p. 174 [II Corinthians 3:6].
165. John Calvin, *Commentaries on Isaiah,* Volume Third, p. 58 [Isaiah 34:16].
166. John Calvin, *Commentaries on the Epistle of Paul the Apostle to the Romans,* translated by John Owen, Grand Rapids, Michigan: Baker Book House, 1979, p. 116 [Romans 3:4].
167. John Calvin, *Commentary on Hebrews,* p. 103 [Hebrews 4:12].
168. John Calvin, *Commentary on Corinthians,* Volume Second, p. 160 [II Corinthians 2:15].

169. John Calvin, *Commentaries on The Catholic Epistles,* translated by John Owen, Grand Rapids, Michigan: Baker Book House, 1979, p. 57 [I Peter 1:23].

170. *Ibid.,* p. 295 [James 1:21].

171. John Calvin, *Commentaries on the Book of the Prophet Ezekiel,* translated by Thomas Myers, Grand Rapids, Michigan: Baker Book House, 1979, p. 108 [Ezekiel 2:2].

172. *The Institutes,* IV.14.6.

173. *Ibid.,* IV.1.1.

174. *The Study of Man,* p. 22.

175. *Ibid.,* p. 24.

176. *Ibid.,* p. 25.

177. *The Institutes,* I.5.14.

178. *The Study of Man,* p. 30.

179. *Ibid.,* p. 31.

180. *Ibid.,* p. 34.

DATE DUE

HIGHSMITH #LO-45220